"As Lindsay de Feliz explains with unflinching honesty in her gutsy follow-up to What About Your Saucepans?, the Dominican Republic takes no prisoners. From the outset, we find the author ensconced in her dusty roadside house with Danilo, her Dominican husband, two stepsons, a dwindling back account, a growing menagerie of cats and dogs and swarms of voracious mosquitos. Things start to look up when they move lock, stock and barrel to the superior sounding 'Pink House', even if the cooker has to be wheeled round to the new house in a wonky wheelbarrow. But when blocked showers, troublesome septic tanks, a stroppy local 'witch' and an unscrupulous vet who moonlights as a taxidermist all take their toll, it becomes clear that this is no ordinary tale about living the dream.

Life After My Saucepans is packed with warmth and infectious humour, even when the clan moves to a pile in the mountains that needs pretty much everything: walls, windows, doors and gates – not to mention an emergency wasp fumigator. We witness in full technicolour the ups and downs of life in Wasp House, the drama and corruption of Dominican politics, the expat women suffering at the hands of their polygamous 'sankies', the lush, mountainous landscapes, the pig-roasts, the traditional Noche Buena feasts and a succession of madcap, local eccentrics. In Chivirico, a five-year-old barefooted boy who proudly announces he will be the author's bodyguard, we get a touching and poignant relationship that tugs at the heartstrings from the outset. And in the end, it's the life-affirming human interest stories that make this book special. Lindsay de Feliz tells it as it is, warts and all, but it's her affection for her adopted country and the people around her that shines through."

Jack Scott, author of *Turkey Street*, jackscott.info

"Fans of What About Your Saucepans? *– the book and the blog – won't be disappointed.* Life After My Saucepans *is another enjoyable and engaging glimpse into life in the Dominican Republic as seen through Lindsay's sympathetic eyes. The setting, the story and the people will come alive in your imagination whether or not you know the country. The simple pleasures and niggling irritations, and the tragedies and triumphs, both great and small, are described with the honesty, empathy and deadpan humour that Lindsay's readers have come to know and love."*

Ilana Benady, co-author of *Expat FAQs: Moving to and Living in the Dominican Republic, Culture Smart: The Essential Guide to Customs & Culture in the Dominican Republic*, and *Aunt Clara's Dominican Cookbook*

"Lindsay's new book is a combination of amusing adventures and sorrowful occurrences. The book carries forward the story of her new life in the Dominican Republic. All is not a 'live happily ever after' fairy tale in the Caribbean paradise as there is always something or someone to trip up our Happy family to try to prevent them from fulfilling their destiny. In the end, though, Love triumphs in the de Feliz (aka Happy) family."

"Read this book to learn what has happened to the Happy (Feliz) family in their new location. Lindsay's personality comes through in her writing. I've never been to the Dominican Republic and, thanks to the realism of Lindsay's writing, I want to visit and see the places she's told us about."

Margarita Vallazza, author of *El Fruto Mezclado – Mixed Fruit*

AMAZON.CO.UK

"This book is a definite must read. Lindsay gives inspiration to us all. ...Fantastic job Lindsay, you have a wonderful talent so please give us more."

Tirado

"This book will have you laughing out loud at some parts and holding back the tears at others. I couldn't put it down. Highly recommended!"

Nicola

AMAZON.COM

"*What About Your Saucepans?*works because of the way she tells it. Seemingly bizarre situations recalled without any hysterics, laced with doses of humour melded with a growing understanding and love of all the things (good and bad) that the Dominican Republic has to offer."

Nicola Cornwell

"Lindsay's real life story about her adopting the Dominican Republic as her new home are both astonishing and inspiring. ...With her descriptions of the people and the country, you will picture everything as though you were present at each moment. Lindsay's love for her husband and the country shine through so brightly. She makes you really understand what life is truly about."

Laura Prevost Martinez

"Through this book alone, there will be a new understanding and appreciation to live your life to the fullest."

Tracy Padilla

"Lindsay has put together the right combination of useful information and first-hand experiences; and has done so in an honest, witty, and compassionate way. However, this is not a dry, dull account of an expat's life (i.e. best spots to eat and live). It is full of touching, shocking, eye-popping, and very funny accounts of what it means to live on this beautiful island. ...Did I mention funny? Boy, did I laugh! I highly recommend it. You won't regret it."

A Quinta

AMAZON.CA

"This book was not what I expected, it was even better!!"

Mary Vucina

"What is uncanny about the book Lindsay has artfully written is how every page you read literally feels like you are there with the people and partaking in the social life. ...You can almost hear the music and smell the smells that are so familiar in Dominican daily life. ...For anyone wanting to lose yourself for a few hours and enjoy a true work of heart, please pick up this book and see what the fuss is about."

DomQueen

SEE MORE REVIEWS AT:

https://www.amazon.co.uk/productreviews/B00BLLIVGW/ref=acr_search_see_all?ie=UTF8&showViewpoints=1

https://www.amazon.com/product-reviews/1909193313/ref=acr_search_see_all?ie=UTF8&reviewerType=avp_only_reviews&showViewpoints=1

LIFE AFTER
MY SAUCEPANS

Lifting the lid on living in the Dominican Republic

By Lindsay de Feliz

Life After My Saucepans: Lifting the lid on living in the Dominican Republic by Lindsay de Feliz

First published Great Britain 2017 by *Springtime Books*

ISBN 978-0-9955027-4-1

Design © Owen Jones Design *owenjonesdesign.com*
All photographs © Lindsay de Feliz
Chapter 5 photograph © Tracy Perez

Quotations used throughout the book are taken from *Desiderata*, Max Ehrmann, 1927

Please note: real names of some people in this book have been changed to protect their privacy. Where real names have been used, the author has done so with permission.

DEDICATION

This book is dedicated to the two most important men in my life. Danilo, my Dominican husband, my man from Barahona, who I have been with for sixteen years. You may be older and wiser now, but you are still just as cute and still just as infuriating. You make me feel cared for, appreciated, adored and make me laugh and love more than I thought possible. I cannot live without you.

And to Chivirico, my bodyguard. You have shown me the unbridled pleasure a child can bring into a woman's life, something I had never have experienced until you showed me. You bring joy to all you come into contact with, and I cannot wait to see what adventures life will bring you.

ACKNOWLEDGMENTS

So many people have supported me over the past six years since I wrote *What About Your Saucepans?*

First and foremost my mother. She is always there – daily Skype calls, financial help when needed – and I simply could not have coped without her. My sister, Elisabeth, and her husband Gary, and other family members who have always been there for me too.

Online friends have been amazing, especially as I live in the middle of nowhere they are my link with civilisation: Shirley, Tracy, Michelle, Grace, Marge, Robyn, Ro, Heather, Theresa, Olga, all of the men called John, Catherine, thank you for all your support and to all the wonderful ladies from DR Sisterhood – thank you for your appreciation of what I do.

Thanks to Dolores from DR1, Ilana, Avon, Jonathan, Conor, Michael and Lisa for giving me work and helping to keep the wolf from the door.

My great friends in Cacique who have welcomed this *"Americana"* as they call me, into their world, especially Angela, *la Bruja*, who helped me in all my times of crisis, especially with dead animals.

All of those who have provided me, Danilo, and Chivirico with clothes, and with kitchen equipment and the all important British foods such as Oxo cubes, Bisto, Birds Custard Powder,

Cadbury's Chocolate, cheese, walnut whips, Branston pickle, horseradish and pickled onions – I thank you from the bottom of my heart.

Major thanks go to my editor, Jane Dean, to Jack Scott of Springtime Publishing and Jo Parfitt at Summertime Publishing for agreeing to publish this sequel.

The three 'J's' are a formidable team who worked quickly and efficiently to pull my scribblings into a real live book. Jack, among many other things, was responsible for the strap line of the book, Jo speaks little, but when she does it is truly incisive, and exactly on point, and Jane's attention to detail and ability to get things done quickly and perfectly is mind blowing. They really are a joy to work with. Owen, the designer, was the natural choice having worked on *What About My Saucepans?* and once again he did a superb job. Thanks so much to you all.

TABLE OF CONTENTS

PREFACE

FOR THOSE OF YOU WHO HAVE READ MY FIRST BOOK, *What About Your Saucepans?*, you will know everything that's happened to me in the previous ten years, from 2001 to 2011, so you can curl up on the sofa, get yourself a nice cup of tea – or something a little stronger – and prepare once again to enter my life for the next few years.

For those of you who have not read the first book, it is probably cheeky of me to ask you to read it before getting stuck into this one, but being cheeky has never held me back. I promise you this book will make much more sense if you read *What About Your Saucepans?* before *Life After My Saucepans*. However, if you would rather not read it, here is a quick synopsis. I will make it short so as not to bore those of you who have been kind enough to have read it already.

I am Lindsay, British, and I used to have a high-flying job in London. I left my job, my home and my British husband in 2001, when I was forty-five, to travel the world as a scuba diving instructor. I eventually arrived in the Dominican Republic – having been to the Maldives, Singapore, Thailand, Borneo and Menorca – where I met a Dominican man, married him and brought up two of his three boys.

I gave up scuba diving when I was shot through the throat during a burglary, then my husband ran for mayor in the local town of Guayacanes, on the south coast, and lost due to major corruption. We lost everything in the process including our home and business, which were taken from us illegally. Fearing for our lives we left the area and ended up in a *barrio*, or neighbourhood, in a Dominican town far from the tourist and expat enclaves. There we were struggling on very little income and while 1 was writing and translating he went to university, studying to be a lawyer.

There, that's it so everyone should be up to date. Now let's get on with the next part of the story. Will 1 be shot again? Will he run for mayor again? Will we stay in the *barrio*? Will we get our house and business back? What adventures will 1 have? All will be revealed.

CHAPTER ONE

THE PINK HOUSE

---

*"Go placidly amid the noise and haste, and remember
what peace there may be in silence."*
Desiderata, Max Ehrmann 1927

SO WHERE WERE WE? WELL, THE DATE WAS BY NOW SEPTEMBER 2011, and the place was the Dominican Republic. I was living in the *barrio* in Esperanza – in the northwest of the Dominican Republic – along with my husband Danilo and his two boys, my stepsons, Alberto and Dany, where we were just about surviving on very little money. A *barrio* is literally translated as a neighbourhood. Each town is made up of different *barrios*, a collection of homes, some are up-market *barrios* and some are places too dangerous for those who don't live there to walk about in. Our barrio was called *Barrio de Fe* meaning the 'Neighbourhood of Faith' and the town name – Esperanza – means Hope. Pretty apt for what we had been through.

We were in the *barrio,* living downstairs in our rented apartment, with the Dominican landlady living upstairs, when she visited from New York, and whilst I originally loved the place as it seemed like a safe haven after all we had been through, it was becoming a tad annoying. The street outside was a dirt track so the house was always full of dust when it was sunny and full of mud when it rained. It didn't matter how much I mopped or swept (*weesped* as Danilo said), the place was always dirty. The road was also one of the main thoroughfares in the area and so busy and noisy – kids constantly encouraging the dogs to bark, and a stream of vendors broadcasting their wares through loud speakers. There was music from stereos from every house, behind, to the side and in front, for what seemed like twenty-four hours a day and geese wandering up and down honking at anything worth honking at.

The final straw – on top of the noise and the dust – was the problem with the water. Water is something I have always taken for granted. You turn on the tap and out it comes – always. In the previous house in Juan Dolio, on the south coast of the country, we had a well, and unless the electricity was off and the pump didn't work, there was always water. There was a slight problem in that it was a bit smelly at times, such as when a cat fell in and we didn't discover it for a week, but there was always water.

In this house in the *barrio*, we had proper water from the street, which is a lot more hygienic and it arrived every day for an hour or so. It went into a cistern, which was in the back garden, and from there into the house and some of it somehow went up to a big black tank on the roof, which is known as a *tinaco*. The idea is that if the cistern empties for any reason, the *tinaco* should be full and the water will come out of the taps easily because of gravity. The system usually worked perfectly and the landlord had told us the street water hardly ever went off. Dominican truth yet again – the street water did go off a lot, in fact two or three days every week, so we relied a lot on the *tinaco*.

Once the street water went off for two whole weeks as they were scrubbing out the main supply tanks with bleach to get rid of cholera, which was a comforting thought. The other advantage with the *tinaco* was that as it was on the roof, the water was heated by the sun and so it was warm. Although I could put up with most things, I really did not do cold showers. When we arrived in the apartment there was no hot water and the cost of putting in an electric hot water tank was prohibitive for us.

"Danilo, I need warm water for a shower. For a *ducha*. I know it's hot outside, but I cannot stand this freezing cold water," I announced, having just shocked myself awake with an icy shower.

"I has plan. There is thing, *una vaina*, you put on *ducha* at top and it has 'lectric and it make water hot," he replied confidently. "It not cost *mucho*. I go buy."

I had no idea what he was talking about, but a few hours later he returned together with Felipe the portly, beer-loving, electrician. They took off the rusty metal shower head and replaced it with a big white plastic one, and Felipe explained there was an electric filament inside and you just got into the shower, turned a knob on the plastic shower head to warm or hot, it would start buzzing and the water came out hot. It worked! The idea of water, with Dominican electricity, and plastic all together filled me with trepidation and I was tempted to have a shower wearing rubber boots just in case. However, it worked well for a couple of months until the buzzing noise got louder and louder and one day it melted and fell into the bathtub. Back to cold water.

Anyway, there we were with our *tinaco* but it was overflowing all the time as I assume there was no ballcock and so when water started to pour down the roof we had to turn off the pipe, which fed it from the cistern.

One day I noticed that even when I turned the knob it was still leaking water.

"Danilo, the *tinaco* is leaking even though I've turned the tap off."

"No problem, I fix," he replied, and knowing he was not a 'stitch in time saves nine' sort of person I phoned Robert, the landlady's son, who was in charge of sorting things.

"*Hola*, the *tinaco* is leaking," I said.

"No problem," he said, and proceeded to ignore me just as Danilo had done.

A week later, we had no water. None at all, so I called Robert again and he appeared on his clapped-out scooter. Robert was a smart looking chap, always well dressed and he was often seen zooming around the *barrio*. He appeared to have a certain status although I wasn't sure why, and he loved trying to practice his English with me.

"The *tinaco* is empty because it is leaking," I told him.

"I will connect an electric pump to pump the water up to the *tinaco*," he said. Danilo was standing next to him nodding his head in agreement.

"Exactly. That is exactly what we need," Danilo announced.

"There is no point doing that," I retorted. "It's a total waste of time as the bloody *tinaco* is leaking."

Robert looked at Danilo and Danilo looked at Robert grinning all over his face, and they both said together, "*extranjeros*," which means 'foreigners', and shook their heads at my apparent lack of knowledge.

Robert totally ignored me and spent all day sorting out the pump. He set it up to pump for a couple of hours, but we still had no water. I was beginning to feel a tad smug, wandering around with a knowing grin on my face. The next day he returned and climbed on the roof.

"The *tinaco* is leaking," he announced.

"Really, well that is a surprise," I said, trying not to celebrate as Danilo glared at me, daring me with a look not to open my mouth again.

The next day Robert returned with PVC glue stuff in a tube, mended the *tinaco*, pumped the water and hey presto the *tinaco* started to fill up.

I was becoming increasingly frustrated with the location and issues with the apartment, and having come to terms with the fact we were unlikely to get our house in Juan Dolio back in the short term, and having no desire to return there anyway, it was time to find another house to rent.

On the one hand it is not easy to find a house to rent as there are no signs outside and no listings in local papers, but if you put the word out you are looking, a constant stream of people appear who take you to various houses, all hoping you will rent theirs and they then receive commission from the owners.

Everyone wanted Danilo and I and the boys to live in their rented home, or near them. It was the same in Juan Dolio, everyone adored Danilo, and it took only a few weeks for him to be Mr. Popular in the *barrio*. He always had a cheeky grin on his face, would be followed around by the kids like the Pied Piper, helped the old folk to get around, and would always go and visit them. He had this amazing magnetism, which people could not help but be attracted by.

In the end, it took around a month to find the right house. Nice and spacious, my first ever en-suite bathroom, guest room, room for the boys, lovely outside terrace where Danilo could work, surrounded by concrete and not mud, and high walls all around. There was plenty of space for the dogs and it was in a much quieter area.

It took us four days to move, as, unlike England, you do not pack things neatly in labelled boxes, which are then collected by a professional removal company. Everything was thrown in my Jeep, beds and sofas were balanced precariously on the top with guys standing on the sides holding onto them. Things which were too big or too heavy for the Jeep were carried – the cooker was wheeled round to the new house in a wheelbarrow. I stayed at the new house to arrange things there, and to save me stressing out as I saw how things were thrown in the Jeep.

The tiny little fridge arrived safely, but they did not take anything out of it and so it was full of ketchup and mayonnaise, soy sauce and melted butter dripping out of the open door as if some horrendous murder had taken place inside the fridge. The packet of sprouts I had miraculously found and was saving for Christmas was open and a trail of soggy green sprouts followed the route of the fridge from the old house to the new – to the delight of the geese who ran honking along the road following the fridge, just stopping now and then to gobble down my Christmas sprouts.

The back fell off the washing machine and the top from the wardrobe went missing, as did the screws to put the wardrobe doors back on. In true Dominican fashion that was sorted by taking screws from the coffee maker and unscrewing knobs from drawers so the wardrobe doors could be put back on. Now we have knob-less drawers.

So, we were installed in the pink house. It was very, very pink. Pink walls, pink roof, less noise, less dust, but the problems did not vanish overnight.

The inverter for the electricity and all the batteries were moved, as the new house was on the same electrical circuit as the former apartment with only eight hours maximum per day of electricity. However, for some reason whenever we were on inverter power the cursor on my laptop went crazy, flying all over the screen by itself and I often had a shock when I touched the laptop. It was time to call Felipe the portly electrician again.

"Hey Felipe, it is Lindsay, *La Gringa*. There is a problem with the electricity here, can you come and check it out please?"

Felipe turned up within minutes on his scooter, bottle of *Presidente* beer in hand, and baggy jeans hanging half-way down his ample backside. He wandered around sticking some sort of yellow machine into the plug sockets.

"You have problem in that the house, she has no earth. But she has two live wires, one where it should be, and one in the earth outlet. Is easy to fix, you esnap off the earth prong from you plug."

"But I thought it was important to have an earth?" I said, somewhat concerned.

Felipe shrugged his shoulders, so I esnapped off my earth prongs and problem fixed.

The second problem was the shower in the bathroom used by Dany and Alberto, which was blocked and the water would not drain away. It was lovely they had their own bedroom and bathroom, as Dany was by now twenty-one and Alberto nineteen, and neither were working. They loved the *barrio* and would spend most days wandering around talking to people, once they had finished cleaning the house or lying on their double bed in the back room listening to music, or dancing to rap music clutching their crotches with one hand and waving the other hand pointing at an imaginary audience.

"Alberto, go and buy a plunger thingy," I instructed him. "All you have to do is use that and whatever is blocking the drain will get unblocked. And if that doesn't work then get a bit of wire down there as something must be stuck."

"No plunchy thing," interrupted Danilo. "We call landlord."

The landlord turned up, who was the owner's brother, Rafael, as the owner of the house was in New York or *Nueva Yol* as they call it. He pooh poohed the plunger option, which was no surprise to me, as I was beginning to realize that in this part of the world the *Gringa* knew nothing.

"The problem is the pipe, from shower to the road. We need to put in new pipe so will dig up old pipe and put in new pipe then put new concrete in garden. My brother in *Nuevo Yol* will pay for this."

From what I could work out, there appeared to be two types of waste water; *agua negra* (black water) from the toilet, which went into a septic tank, and plain old dirty water from the sink or shower or washing machine which went through pipes out into the street. Everyone had the same system and the streets were constantly full of water peppered with bits of rice and the odd bean and on washing day there were bubbles and foam all over the place. Maybe that is why there were so many mosquitoes and so many cases of dengue fever in the area.

Anyway, the so-called plumbers descended on us, broke up the concrete with pickaxes and laid new pipe. However, what a surprise, the shower was still blocked. In the end they got a piece of wire, shoved it down the plughole in the shower and pulled out a plastic toy. I said not a word. The shower worked perfectly, but alas, that was not the end of the story.

Rafael climbed up onto the flat concrete roof.

"I think there is still a problem. *Si*, it is the septic tank," he announced. Do not ask me how he came to that conclusion. He insisted on opening the septic tank, which was concreted in, so out came the pickaxes again. He prised open the tank, which was full of what looked like dirty water. Now this tank had been emptied a month earlier, just before we moved in, and they should only need emptying every several years, not months. In fact, if it works really well it should last a lifetime. I went to find Danilo.

"Danilo, explain to me how septic tanks work, please." I had never given much thought to where poo went, as in England it just goes somewhere, but I realised now I needed some education on the subject.

"The tank he is full of water. There is peep at the top and water he go out in peep."

"Where to?"

"Jus out. Then the cheet she go into bottom."

"Cheet? Oh, shit. And what happens when she is at the bottom?"

"She.....," he wrinkled his brow, "she poof." He splayed his fingers.

"Right. She disappears. The sheet disappears. How?"

"*No se*. I no know. Sheet go into bottom and poof. Maybe insec eat sheet."

Clear as mud then, but Danilo said they are supposed to be full, but the landlord was having none of it and called the local septic tank emptying service, which happened to be none other than Robert, our ex-landlady's son. He arrived in a van this time with his special sheet sucking pipes and sucked the septic tank dry. I thought that was the end of the matter, but no.

It was decided the walls of the septic tank were being invaded by palm tree roots and those roots were transporting rainwater into the sewage tank. Basically the reverse of everything I thought I knew, in that roots transport water to the tree, not the tree uses roots to pipe water into septic tanks.

The group of four or five saggy-jeaned and craggy-faced men prepared to cut down the palm trees, four brandishing machetes and one an axe. Luckily, they were dissuaded from that and I became aware of their next plan when I went to our bathroom to use the toilet. The toilet had gone. Totally vanished. There was nothing there. Where the toilet had once been there was just a little porcelain stump about four inches tall, which was impossible to perch on. I went outside with my legs crossed.

"Err, has anyone seen the toilet?"

"The toilet has too much water in it. We need to buy new toilet," replied Rafael, and off he went carrying my toilet under his arm. He returned with a new toilet, which took two days to fit, the septic tank was sealed and everyone was happy.

I still have absolutely no idea what the problem was, nor how removing a perfectly functioning toilet and replacing it with the same model has solved anything, but Danilo thinks Rafael wanted a new toilet and this way he got one for nothing.

I quickly got to know the neighbours. Everyone had the same name – *vecina*, which means female neighbour or *vecino*, which is the male equivalent. On the left was a very odd woman who had been away visiting her daughter for a while and someone had stolen the water pipes to her house. I called her 'the witch' as she looked like a witch, long, dirty, unkempt hair, long frilly skirts and baggy stained T-shirts. She spoke like a witch as well, in a high pitched, annoying semi-screaming voice and would yell, *"Hola mi amor"* at me every time she passed. I wasn't her bloody love.

Understandably she was a tad miffed about the lack of pipes, so she bought some new pipes and the *vecino* from over the road dug up the road and put the pipes in for her. We called him cockman as he bred fighting roosters, or cockerels, and spent most of the day sitting outside his hut on a dirty, old plastic chair stroking his fighting cock. He also had no toilet in his hut so I would often see him standing up against the side wall having a pee.

I wasn't convinced he was a qualified plumber as he dug a channel in the road with his machete, and stuck the pipes together using the flame from a candle. Anyway, problem solved one would think. No. She didn't have the money for enough pipes, so the pipe stopped outside our gate and didn't reach to her house. He fitted a tap there and when she wanted water she came out in front of the gate and turned on the tap. Once more of the neighbours realised there was a standpipe close by, there was a steady stream of people filling up a range of containers. However, there were two problems. Firstly, many people didn't bother turning the tap off which meant there was a constant lake outside the gate and secondly, we could not get the car out as the standpipe was right in the middle of the exit from the driveway.

Despite the frustration with the locals and the way things were done, life was good and full of laughs. Danilo continued to look after me and do everything he could to make life as bearable as possible, as did the boys, so however hard it was I felt spoiled. The boys would do all the cleaning and they and Danilo shared most of the cooking. We would all take the dogs for a walk through the banana plantations on the other side of the canal, once the heat of the sun had gone for the day. None of them needed to be on a lead once we were away from the street and had crossed the rickety bridge over the canal just a few minutes away. Tyson, the Great Dane would bound along with his loping stride scaring any Haitian to death who came along on his bicycle taking a short cut home through the banana fields. We would pick fruit off the trees overhanging the path, mangos, limes, sour oranges and together laugh about the events of the day.

However, life continued to be hard. The fridge was tiny and not connected to the inverter as it would use too much power from the batteries, which meant it was disconnected for up to eighteen hours a day. Hardly worth keeping anything in it so shopping was done daily at the local *colmado* run by José. Every morning I would pick my way between the puddles and the rubbish in the street and walk up to the *colmado*. I would wave to Lala, the neighbour who lived to the right of the house, who was always sitting in the front porch of her little wooden hut. Lala was in her eighties she thought, with a round face and round body and her dark greying hair scraped back into a bun.

Every morning, at around 6am, she wandered past my

house in her nightie to go to the *colmado* to get a little packet of coffee. If she didn't have the money for a little packet of coffee, which was called a *sobre* and cost RD$6, about eight pence or thirteen cents, she stopped at my gate and yelled *"Vecina"* handing over her mug and I had to go and get her a mug of coffee from my coffee maker, with four sugars. She complained if it didn't have enough sugar.

Lala was diabetic. She was insulin controlled and had a cracked mug with the syringe in it kept on a rickety wooden table outside the back door, together with the insulin in a little bottle. Her husband gave her the injections every day. She had no idea how much she should have and nor did he as she had no sugar testing machine. In addition, she couldn't see very well, maybe due to the diabetes, and had a cataract in one eye, so could not see out of it at all. Luckily, a cataract in the other eye had been operated on by a team of American doctors who came to the *barrio* a few years ago. She was waiting for them to return to do the other eye.

"Hey, fideito," she would shout at me as I walked passed. That means 'little noodle' which she called me as I was thin. "Call in on your way back. I have something for you."

On the way back from the *colmado* I would always sit and chat to her for a few minutes, and she would hand me a lettuce, or half a cabbage, as one of her twelve children had a vegetable truck. Most of her kids lived in *Nueva Yol*, but three or four lived locally. Sometimes we would sit together companionably shucking peas, or cleaning rice, while she told me about life in the Dominican Republic in the past. I loved listening to her stories about what life was like fifty years ago.

"People liked Trujillo, the one they now say was a dictator," she would explain. "He was the president in the Fifties and Sixties and in those days you could go to sleep in the middle of the road with money in your pocket and no one would take it. There was no crime, not like all these delinquents today."

"But I thought he was a bad man?" I asked. "He murdered people if they didn't agree with him, like the Butterflies, the *Mariposa* sisters?"

"Well, yes," she agreed. "You had to lock up your daughters, especially if they were beautiful, but for us, living here, life was good."

The *colmado* did not have a big choice of food, so every day was the same. Mashed plantains, called *mangu*, with scrambled eggs and onions, or salami. Some days we had chicken, rice and beans and sometimes I would make a chicken curry. We were often hungry, especially towards the end of the month as the money ran out, and sometimes I thought I would scream if I had to eat another bloody plantain. But there was no choice, and never enough money to go to a real supermarket and buy something nice like a piece of real cheese rather than soap masquerading as cheese. Alberto did most of the cooking and the cleaning, leaving Danilo free to study and me free to write. Dany split his time between our house and Juan Dolio, some five or six hours away by bus. He had a child with a woman there before we left, although it appeared he had split up with the child's mother shortly after Danilo lost the election. I really thought the boys should find work to help contribute to our meagre finances, but although they tried, there were simply no jobs available.

Alberto seemed to be out a lot, he was now nineteen going on twenty and had been looking for work, but there was nothing to be found. One evening he came over to me as I was typing away on the computer.

"Lindsay, I have girlfren. I bring her now to mee you."

"What?" It all seemed a little odd to have a formal presentation, but that is how it worked in the *barrio*. The first meeting was apparently very important.

Alberto stood there wringing his hands.

"What's the matter?" I asked.

"You mus not say bad things abow me. No tell she I no clean bedroom. No tell she things from many time ago when I was chilren. Okay?"

I laughed. "Sure I won't say anything bad. No worries."

At around ten o'clock that night, Alberto walked in holding the hand of a tall attractive girl. Alberto was now over six-foot tall and she was only a little shorter than him. She had long dark hair, was slim and dressed in the traditional tight Dominican jeans and tight T-shirt.

I jumped up from my chair, took off my glasses, fluffed up my hair, and nervously held out my hand.

"Hi, you must be Ana," I said. "Danilo, come here and meet Ana," I shouted, as he was in the bedroom watching television.

"So sorry about the mess, it's the puppy, Meg, she's wrecking the place," I apologized, wringing my hands. I looked around horrified at the chewed up empty toilet roll inserts, and bits of paper all over the place. And then, horror of horrors, spotted a little puddle of lemon-coloured puppy piddle. I managed to manoeuvre myself expertly in front of it.

"And, Ana, do you do anything?" I asked, somewhat stupidly.

She replied in perfect English, "I'm at university, studying to be a teacher."

Luckily Danilo then appeared, as I was running out of things to say.

"Hello, nice to meet you. At least my son has good taste in women!"

Alberto could see things were not going to get any better and said this was only the informal introduction and a formal one would follow shortly. He ushered her out as rapidly as he could.

"Danilo," I said, once they had left, "what is a formal introduction?"

"Well, we have something to eat and talk more," he replied.

In Britain we would have a nice pot of tea and cucumber sandwiches with the crusts off and fruitcake or a Victoria sponge cake, but I have no idea here. Whatever it is I will have to do it well. This is the woman who will feed me mashed plantains when I lose my teeth and change my incontinence pads when I am old and decrepit.

The days fell into a pattern. I would get up early, around 5.30am or 6am, shower and dress in jeans and a T-shirt and sit down at my computer, which was on at little table at the front window in the house, only a few feet from the road. There was a small terrace in front of the window where the dogs would sit. Tyson the Great Dane was fit and well, but Fred had died of cancer and Sophie of some mysterious illness. The local vet, Francis, was appalling. He was very overweight and his surgery was disgusting, with scraps of bloody tissue and rags all over the place, instruments shoved in a drawer and cages of birds piled higgledy-piggledy on top of each other. When you went there were often groups of young lads betting on Siamese Fighting Fish which lined the walls in dirty jam jars. Francis said he was qualified, but seemed to know nothing. He also worked as an animal stuffer – taxidermist. You would take a sick dog to him and leave it there for treatment and he would say it died. However, he would often cure them and sell them, or worse, stuff them. You had no way of knowing. He was unable to treat

Fred or Sophie, having no idea what the problem was, and often the injections he gave were just water. We had acquired a new dog, half Rottweiler and half Chow Chow, neither of which breeds I liked. She was small and brown and looked neither like a Rottie nor a Chow, but Danilo wanted us to have more dogs for protection. We named her Meg – after Meg Ryan – and she was a total pain in the arse from day one. She threw up in the car all the way back from Sosúa, where we went to collect her, and refused to live outside with the other dogs. In fact, she spent most of her time under our bed.

Francis had called Danilo and said he had a big dog to give him, and as Danilo loved big dogs he took it. It was an English Mastiff. Absolutely enormous, and he had spent his whole life in Santiago zoo in a tiny little cage. He had massive black growths on his elbows, from lying on concrete all his life, and was totally blind, and Danilo fell in love with him. His name was Mammoo meaning 'mammoth', but we rechristened him Sumo which lasted ten minutes because he was always bumping into things which resulted in me saying, "Oh you silly boy," and Silly Boy stuck.

All ten of the cats had moved with us from the apartment, apart from Zebedee One. We had Zebedee One and Two, neutered ginger toms and the sons of Matilda, the original cat. Although the cats were all brought round in cat baskets, no one could find Zeb One, but given the previous house wasn't far away, just next to the *colmado* I went to every day. I thought I could keep an eye out for him and bring him to the new house. I did see him a couple of times, once with his brother, Zeb Two, back at the old house, and once or twice he came to visit us at the new house when his brother brought him round, but he never stayed.

One day I was sitting at the computer and I heard a cat yowling and the dogs barking outside – a sound I knew all too well and I rushed outside to see Zebedee One being viciously attacked by the dogs. They had him backed up against the wall and there was no escape. I screamed at the dogs and tried hitting them with the broom and eventually Zeb managed to get away and go under my Jeep – right nearby. I knelt down by the Jeep and pulled him out and took him inside. He was dreadfully injured so I just laid him in my lap.

"Zeb, I am soo sorry," I sobbed as I was stroking him, thinking he could not have been eating well as he seemed much thinner than I remembered. He died within seconds. I called Alberto and Danilo, who were at Ana's house over the road and they came back.

"Can you bury him, please? And somewhere nice."

"Well," declared Alberto, "we can't bury him here as there is no earth, it's just concrete."

"Take him and bury him in the banana plantation the other side of the canal then. And do it properly, with respect," I warned, wagging my finger at him.

Alberto put Zeb in a plastic bag and set off for the banana plantation. I didn't understand why the dogs had gone for him, as he had never had any problems with them before, but I shrugged the thought out of my mind and went back to work. By now I was getting so used to animals dying that, while upset of course, I seemed to have adapted to the Dominican way of coping with death, which was allowing yourself to feel the pain of the loss for a short while and then totally block it out. This ability was to serve me well in the months and years to come.

The following day I set off for the *colmado* as usual and as I approached it one of the neighbours from where we used to live stopped me.

"Hi, Lindsay, I see your cat hasn't found his way to your new house yet."

"No, and he won't be," I replied ruefully. "The dogs killed him yesterday."

"Err, I don't think so," she said, with a puzzled look on her face. "I've just seen him in the garden of your old place with his brother, the other Zebedee."

"What!!" and I rushed to look in the garden and there they both were. *What on earth was going on? How had Zebedee risen from the dead?*

I continued wandering to the *colmado*, feeling a mixture of excitement and confusion, bought the supplies for the day and then walked hurriedly back down the street, looking forward to telling Danilo the news. As I walked past Lala's house she yelled at me, "Have you seen my cat?"

"Cat?" I asked. "I didn't know you had a cat."

"Yes, a big ginger one. He's always here, but I haven't seen him since yesterday afternoon. Can you let me know if you see him wandering around in your garden?"

"Of course I will. But I haven't seen him wandering around," I said, crossing my fingers behind my back.

I walked quickly back to the house, to find Danilo and Alberto sitting outside in the covered gazebo at the table.

"Guess what?" I announced. "Zebedee One is alive, I've just seen him at the old house."

Alberto looked stunned. "But he was definitely dead when I threw him in the canal, and I tied the plastic bag up so he can't have got out. Can he?" So much for a nice burial in the banana plantation.

My life seemed to be a series of events, both amusing and not so amusing, amidst the struggle to survive, but the constant in all of this was Tyson. The gorgeous Great Dane who had been with us through thick and thin, who was a friend to all who knew him, who shook paws with everyone, sat next to me as I worked or wrote all day. He was approaching his seventh birthday and lying on the floor next to me, when suddenly he tried to get up and couldn't. His back legs just stayed on the floor and he yelped in confusion and pain as he tried to move. I ran to him and tried to lift him, but he couldn't stand at all. He peed all over the floor and looked at me distraught with his big brown eyes as if he was asking, "What the hell is happening to me?" He was in obvious pain, so I called the idiotic useless vet Francis to come over and at the same time tried to Google and ask friends what it was likely to be.

It appeared that Great Danes were prone to suffer from embolisms in the spinal cord, which rendered them paralyzed. It was incurable, although had we been in a First World country he could have had MRI scans and been hospitalized and had physiotherapy. As it was he only had us, Google and useless Francis,

Francis arrived. "Let me hoist him into my truck and I'll take him back to the surgery and treat him there, I can sort this, no problem."

"Over my dead body," I said in English, knowing he couldn't understand and smiling sweetly as I said it. "I don't think so Francis, I would rather keep him here, and I don't think it is wise to move him. Can you just give him an anti-inflammatory injection please? And a pain killer?" I paused and had second thoughts. "Let me get Alberto to go and buy it at the pharmacy."

The problem with Francis is he would inject water and charge you for it. Alberto returned with the injection, which was given to Tyson who was unable to move.

We tried for four days, but he was no better. He peed and pooed where he lay and was obviously so uncomfortable and it was heartbreaking watching him try desperately to walk, pulling his one-hundred-and-forty pounds along with only his front paws. In the end, we felt had no choice and on his seventh birthday Danilo took him to be put to sleep. I had become hardened to my animals dying as it happened all too often, but in the case of Tyson I was unable to stem the wave upon wave of desolation. I was heartbroken and had lost the last real link with our old home.

The house was terribly quiet and empty without Tyson; he had filled every room with his presence. We had Silly Boy and the little addition Meg, but I couldn't help scouring the Internet to see if I could find another Great Dane. No dog could replace him, but I had fallen in love with the breed.

Eventually I found a German breeder who had a female, the same colour as Tyson, and he swore she had all her pedigree papers. There was no way we could afford the standard US$1,000 for a Great Dane, but he was selling her for only US$200, so we borrowed the cash and Danilo went to pick her up. She was four months old, the size of a small goat, but strangely the German would not meet Danilo at his home, but brought the dog down to the road to meet him. He said he had not had her vaccinated, nor did he have the papers, but would send them. He never did.

Danilo was not in a car, so he waited for the bus. He was near Puerto Plata, some two hours or more from the house, and when the bus arrived they would not let the dog on. He managed to get a motorcycle taxi, holding the puppy, but he would only go so far, and four hours later Danilo arrived at the house having taken one motorcycle taxi after another, with one very confused puppy.

She was black and white, just like Tyson had been, with massive paws and black floppy ears, but she was also covered in sores, fleas and ticks, which we treated slowly but successfully and had her vaccinated – stupidly by Francis. Three months later, Belinda, as we called her, went down with Parvovirus. So much for the vaccine. She lay by my side on a blanket for ten days, almost unconscious when she wasn't vomiting or covering the tiled floor with bloody diarrhoea. Mr. Google came to my aid and daily I went to the *agroveterinaria* to buy medicines, and the man there told me to rehydrate her by injecting large quantities of a saline drip under her skin, which looked like tennis ball sizes of fluid which went down as they were slowly absorbed. After ten days of just lying, not eating, nor moving, not making a sound, she suddenly stood up, wandered into the garden for a pee, then came in looking for food. Cured, to my great relief, and she was soon wandering around the garden, waiting for the ice cream man, bouncing through the banana plantations when we went for a walk and a happy joyful dog.

A year later, Francis died of a drug overdose. There is karma.

CHAPTER TWO

CHIVIRICO, THE BODYGUARD

"Neither be cynical about love; for in the face of all aridity
and disenchantment it is as perennial as the grass."
Desiderata, Max Ehrmann 1927

I WAS SITTING AT MY COMPUTER AS USUAL, LOOKING OUT distractedly through the bars at the window in front of the screen, and I saw a tiny young boy looking in through the fence, which went around the house. Belinda and Silly Boy took no notice of him, and Meg, lying at my feet, did not even raise her head. I was used to the kids stopping and looking at the dogs or asking me for money.

"Dame cinco pesos gringa," they would shout on a regular

basis asking me for five pesos. I smiled at the kid and yelled, *"Hola,"* and he shouted back *"Hola,"* with a cheeky toothless grin on his face and scampered off barefoot down the dirt road. Fifteen minutes later he was back and we went through the same ritual. This time I walked out of the front door and sat down on a low wall, which surrounded the tree in the front garden.

"Hi, what's your name?" I asked him.

"Chivirico," he replied confidently. He was very very small, dressed in a grubby T-shirt and jeans, with no shoes on his feet and the most charming grin I had ever seen on a child.

"How old are you Chivirico?" I asked.

"I am five," he replied. "It is my birthday today".

I reached into my pocket and stretched through the fence and put a ten peso coin into his hand.

"Happy birthday," I said, smiling, and he grinned back, gripped his little fist tightly round the coin and ran off down the road. He was back the next day.

"Hola, it is my birthday today," he shouted through the bars.

"Hmm, it was your birthday yesterday," I reprimanded him.

"I was five yesterday and today is my birthday again so I am six," he replied confidently.

I eventually found out he was five and his birthday was not for another few months in September.

He came to the gate at least ten times a day if not more. Sometimes I would get a break from being inside the shaded but hot house and I would go outside and sit and talk to him. It was stifling hot in the *barrio*, with little or no breeze. When the breeze did pick up, the putrid smell of rotting animals and garbage, piled up in the canal, would drift the hundred yards to the house and linger for a few seconds before thankfully disappearing. The road in front of the house was rutted, brown and dusty, with little tracks of water where the pipes belonging to the witch next door were leaking. The hand-dug gutters down each side were full of dirty water, vegetable peelings, soap suds and rubbish. We were the only concrete house on the street. The rest were wooden shacks, with peeling paint and cockerels strutting across their front porches. Street dogs with no particular homes lay sleeping in the dust on the road, moving reluctantly and slowly when a motorbike or occasional car came past. The sky was usually a deep blue with the occasional white fluffy cloud drifting lazily across. We didn't have many flowers in the garden, just palm trees chock full of coconuts, which would come crashing down every so often. The whole environment seemed dry and arid.

When Chivirico arrived we would chat and sometimes he would shoot me with a plastic pipe and duck back down the wall so I couldn't shoot him back. The ice cream man would come on his bicycle most days and give each of the dogs a five peso ice cream through the bars of the gate and Chivirico would come running down the road as soon as he heard the man ringing his bell, on the pretext of helping with the dogs, but really to get an ice cream himself. One day he was using a twig as a gun shouting, "Bang bang," as he shot me and when the ice cream man came I explained that the twig was a gun. Chivirico looked at me as if I was a total idiot.

"This isn't a gun, it's a twig!"

It took me a while to find out more about him. His real name was Eury which I found very difficult to pronounce – sort of like Yuri without the 'Y' but with a bit of an 'Eee' sound first and he lived with his grandparents just down the road from us, about hundred yards away on the other side of the street, in a little wooden house with a zinc roof and chickens wandering in and out. His grandparents had a few children, one of who was Ana, Alberto's girlfriend, and another was Eury's father. I had no real idea where his mother was, but understood she was in the capital, Santo Domingo, and had left him when he was three weeks old. His father now lived with Lala's daughter and they had two children, born after Eury. I wasn't really sure why Eury lived with his grandparents and not his father and stepmother, but it is common in the Dominican Republic for fathers to keep male children when the relationship breaks up, and also common for the father's parents to take the child. It is also common for stepmothers not to want their husband's children by previous relationships.

Eury was known as Chivirico, which means cheeky, and given how hard I found it to say his real name that is what he was always called. He was amazingly bright even though he had not yet started school and after a couple of weeks of chatting he decided he wanted to be my personal security guard.

He came to the gate one day looking very smart and wearing flip-flops and called me outside.

"You are a foreigner, so you need a security guard, a *watchyman* (as they say it in Spanish). I will work for you and you pay me every fifteen days. I want two hundred pesos every fifteen days and double pay at Christmas." That was around US$5.

"What will you do with the money?" I asked.

"I will use it to buy milk for my brother and sister, and I will give some to my grandma for food."

The deal was struck and every day he stood outside the house guarding it with a twig. If I went to the *colmado* he would walk with me, his little hand grabbing mine tightly, holding a twig in the other for protection, only leaving his post at noon to go home for lunch. We talked about everything, and he was like a sponge soaking it up. He would walk with me when I went shopping and to the bank where he loved seeing the money spitting out of the ATM. He became my shadow, and I began to find myself missing him when he wasn't around.

We didn't have visitors from overseas at the pink house. I don't think most people could cope with the monotony and scarcity of the diet, lack of electricity, the heat and surfeit of mosquitoes. However, none of those things had ever put Heather and Ian off. They came from Canada. Heather was in her thirties, an attractive brown, wavy-haired, slim girl who was a teacher in Canada and had lived near us in Juan Dolio when she was teaching in a school in the *batey* – the sugar cane area – and she lived in very basic accommodation in Consuelo near San Pedro de Macorís. She would come and spend weekends with us where she had hot water, a pool and Indian curries. Both she and Ian, her tall doctor husband, loved the Dominican Republic and had returned for their honeymoon. They were both passionate about the country and helping people who were less well off than them. Rather than do the normal thing of lying on a white sandy beach and staying in a luxury five-star hotel, as they were both fitness fanatics and loved nature, they had decided to climb Pico Duarte, the highest mountain in the Caribbean at just over three thousand metres, which took two or three days, and to come and see me in the pink house.

When they came to see me they also wanted to visit the market at Dajabon, the border crossing from Haiti in the north-west of the country, which is open two days a week and has a bi-national market between Haiti and the Dominican Republic. I had checked Google maps, which said it was seventy-six kilometres away from the pink house and would take an hour and fourteen minutes. Unfortunately, I did not realise that in the same way a Dominican minute is not the same as an English minute, a Dominican kilometre is much longer than an English kilometre.

We set off in the Jeep, which was making odd noises from the front offside wheel and was also very bouncy. The reason for this became apparent some half an hour later when the front offside tyre exploded. This was not a major issue as in this country people stop and help you, which was needed as I had no jack, and within a matter of minutes the spare tyre was on.

Once we reached the town of Santiago Rodriguez we stopped again and Heather and Ian bought me a new spare tyre. I decided to ask the tyre man how much further it was to Dajabon.

"That is forty minutes from here," he replied. Another chap piped up.

"No, it isn't that far. It depends how fast you drive. If you drive fast it is forty minutes but if you drive slowly it is only thirty minutes."

Err, right. We set off driving slowly. Maybe it would have been a little quicker if the road only had cars on it, but we were obviously in the middle of cattle country and kept getting stuck in the middle of herds of beautiful floppy eared cows and it really began to feel as if we were in the back of beyond. The road was full of potholes and old men with donkeys were meandering along. There were very few cars on the road.

Eventually we hit Dajabon after three and a half hours and a hundred and fifty kilometres according to the Jeep's instrument panel. The priority was lunch and a loo, and then we went to find the market. We had no idea where it was, or what it looked like, but we asked where the border crossing was as we knew it would not be far from there. Next to the border gate – on one side of a bridge over the River Massacre, which runs along the border – there was a dirt parking area, with a border guard and his gun standing somewhat menacingly. I drove the Jeep into the rutted parking lot, parked and got out, smiling at the guard. He did not smile back and gripped his shotgun tighter. There was a small, low, badly made fence of posts and barbed wire along the side of the area overlooking the river, which marks the border with Haiti. Heather, Ian and I walked over to the fence with the guard watching our every move.

"Oh, my God," I gasped, and looked around at Heather and Ian, both of whom had instinctively put their hands over their mouths in shock. Eyes wide open and that look on their faces as if they could not comprehend exactly what they were seeing.

The river was some ten to fifteen feet below us and it was full. It was obviously not deep as people were bathing and women were washing clothes and there were mud banks here and there. There must have been close to a hundred people within that small area. Most of them were naked, men, women and children. One little boy, with a distended belly, came walking through the river to below where we were standing.

"*Cinco pesos por favor?*" He held out his outstretched hand asking for only five pesos. Beyond the river there was scrubland with the odd wooden structure and to the left was the bridge over the river, crowded with people lining up to try and get into the Dominican Republic.

It was a most peculiar feeling knowing you were looking at another country and I once again thought there but for the Grace of God I was in my body and not in one of theirs. I had a feeling of desolation looking across at the barren landscape knowing if I wanted to I could go there, but they could not come here.

The guard came over to us and asked us to leave, so we checked out the border control on the Dominican side and then made our way to the market, ending up stuck in long lines of cars, trucks, motorbikes and people before managing to find somewhere to park. The heat inside the Jeep was appalling as we did not want to open the windows, being scared someone would reach in, and there were car horns sounding and people pushing up against the car, clambering over the bonnet and at last we managed to find a parking spot.

I have never seen anything like this market. It was the size of maybe ten football fields, enormous, part outside with a massive blue building at one side, the size of the Royal Albert Hall, with stalls inside, upstairs and down. The first thing to hit you was the smell of sweaty bodies. The stink was appalling and clung to our clothes all the way home. It was hot, very crowded, dusty and crazy. People were rushing everywhere. Women with bags and containers on their heads, yelling what they were selling. Men rushing hither and thither with wheelbarrows, empty and full. People bumping into you, squashing you, pushing you. Most of the people were Haitian – the woman were dressed in long cotton skirts and brightly printed tops, carrying forty-pound bags of flour on their heads, or washing-up bowls filled with peanuts or bottles of bleach, plastic bags, sweet corn, second hand shoes. The men were mainly barefoot, in faded dark-coloured trousers held up with string and wearing dirty, torn, short-sleeved shirts. They pushed wheelbarrows full of bags of cement, of sand, of sugar and washing powder. It was like being in a tsunami of people, being swept in a direction you didn't know if you wanted to go in and had no idea where it was going to.

"Heather, how long do you want to stay here," I shouted above the din, praying she would not say hours.

"Oh, my God. It's terrible. Let's just go into the big blue building and see if it is any better there. Say, ten minutes?"

Ian agreed with her, nodding his head, and clutching our bags tightly to our chests we weaved our way through the crowds into the enormous blue metal structure at the far side.

It was no better inside, except it was in the shade. The stalls were well laid out with piles stacked high of clothes, shoes, bags, electrical goods, food of all descriptions, household goods, cleaning materials, sacks of rice, corn, sugar, everything and anything you could think of. The stallholders were eating, sleeping, lying on piles of rugs, sheets, and blankets. The smell of sweat was still omnipresent and it was an experience I will never forget, but nor will I repeat it. I saw nothing I would want to buy, apart from a small bag of fresh chilli peppers, which were always difficult to find in the *barrio*.

We came home a different route. It took two hours, was a much better road and was a hundred and sixty-five kilometres via Monte Cristi on the north coast. There were no cows, fewer potholes and the landscape was flat, barren and desolate and dotted with cactus plants – the way we had driven earlier was green, lush and mountainous. It always amazes me that this country has such a wide variety of landscapes and microclimates.

As we were on one of the main routes from Haiti into the Dominican Republic it was full of military checkpoints looking for illegal Haitians, illegal guns and drugs. Each time we approached one I could feel my heart pounding in my chest. I am not sure why, as they would have no reason to cause problems, but you can never tell if they will shake you down for money. As it was we were stopped at two out of the five checkpoints. When the stern looking, gun toting, military men wave you down you have no choice but to stop as they have a long plank of wood with nails in, and if you don't look like you are stopping they put it on the road and you say goodbye to a tyre or two. The first guy who stopped us was nice and after a couple of questions let us continue, but the second was very threatening and suspicious of the fact we did not have passports on us. I handed over my Dominican identity card (*cedula*), but he wanted to see my residency permit which I did not have with me. In the end he, too, let us go.

We eventually arrived home, dirty, smelly and sunburned and Chivirico came running down the road to open the gate with a big grin on his face. He had been waiting and watching for hours.

I arrived home and pondered on the fact I was the proud owner of a bag of chillies. To buy these chillies had taken eight hours in total, fifteen hundred pesos in petrol, three hundred pesos in tips for changing the wheel, sixteen hundred pesos for a new tyre, sixty pesos in bottles of water, four hundred and fifty pesos for lunch, and twenty-five pesos to people with ropes across the street asking for money for a street party, leading to a grand total of three thousand six hundred and thirty-five pesos or not far off US$100 – all paid for by Heather and Ian. Plus the twenty pesos for the chillies themselves.

I cooked an Indian curry with the chillies. They were the hottest I have ever eaten in my entire life. The market at Dajabon had its revenge.

Chivirico loved coming to the bank with me and was totally fascinated by the ATM machine. He would put the card in, then crouch down a little with his hand ready to take the money out when it appeared, all the time staring intently as he was listening to the whirring of the money being counted. He would then not want to come home, wanting to watch more people using the machine and the money being spewed out.

"I need a bank card, so the machine will give me money too," he announced determinedly.

"Well, to have a card you need a bank account and to open an account you need money," I explained. "This money is my money, not the bank's money. They just look after it for me to stop *ladrones* or thieves taking it from the house."

"Well, I will open an account – I just need to make the money."

From then on his sole purpose was earning money to open a bank account. He was by now at school in the mornings, but as soon as he had had his lunch he would come running down the road to do jobs. He washed the car for twenty pesos, fed the dogs for ten pesos, learned how to bake and cook and would make biscuits, brownies, fried yuca balls with cheese, *kipes* – like falafels, *empanadas* – meat or cheese wrapped in pastry and fried, and other Dominican snack food, and take them round the neighbourhood to sell on a plastic tray balanced on his head. Everything had to be laid out nicely on the tray and there were even serviettes for his clients.

However, there was a problem as each time he would get paid a few pesos he would go straight away to the *colmado* to spend them on a biscuit or sweets.

"Chivirico, if you keep spending all your money you won't have any to put in the bank," I admonished him.

"I am hungry, and it is more important to eat than to put money in the bank. You cannot save money when you are hungry, so when I am not hungry I can save it."

The discussion continued over a game of dominoes.

"Listen, if you earn ten pesos why not spend five pesos on a biscuit and put five pesos to one side for the bank. That way you aren't hungry and you are saving."

"Good idea," he nodded, and a couple of days later he had fifteen pesos and insisted we go to the bank the next day to open the account.

The next morning arrived and once school was over Chivirico came running to the house as usual.

"We can't go to the bank today as my dad took ten of my fifteen pesos to give five pesos each to my brother and sister. He said it is important to share, which I know is true, so I will have to make more money today. What shall we cook? "

I was amazed he was so calm about it and by the end of the day he had eleven pesos, having spent some on a biscuit at the *colmado*, so the following day off we went to the bank, him with his eleven pesos clutched tightly in his hand.

We arrived there during lunch hour and so the bank was nearly empty. Chivirico sat down at the customer service desk and put his eleven pesos on the desk in front of the smartly dressed, smiling clerk.

"I want a bank account and a card that I can put in the machine please," he announced.

The bank employee smiled and said, "You need more money than that. You need at least five hundred pesos, (around £10GBP) and as a child you can't have a card – you have a special book instead. You must also have an adult's name on the book and you can put money in, but they have to take money out. Come back with who will open the account with you, your birth certificate and five hundred pesos".

"Oh," said Chivirico. "Okay, well, I will have to save very hard and cook lots more things and wash lots of cars. I need money to buy a Jeep and Lindsay needs a new oven as she burns my cakes sometimes." Again he seemed unfazed and we walked home making plans on how to make five hundred pesos. Once we arrived at the house he made a money box out of a Gatorade bottle, and I told him when it was full we could go back to the bank and open his account.

At last Chivirico's Gatorade pot reached the magic number of RD$500 and off we went to the bank. I had thought long and hard about who should be the custodian of his account. If it were me we would be sure no money would be taken out, but on the other hand I doubted I would be living there forever, and then how would he get money out, and I didn't want his family to think I didn't trust them.

In the end we decided the account manager should be his aunt Ana.

We were in the middle of the passing of Hurricane Sandy so when the rain stopped for a short while, together the three of us squelched our way through the muddy streets to the bank with Chivirico clutching his Gatorade pot. After a long wait we sat down to open the account. He could barely contain his excitement. As usual it took ages with all the paperwork, but at last it was done, and he walked out holding his account book with pride.

It was now November and as it was both my and Danilo's birthdays, Chivirico came up to me and said something I would hear a lot over the next few years. By now he called me De Fe (pronounced Fay) a lot, as that is what Danilo always called me.

"De Fe. I have an idea."

Here we go, I thought, *another Chivirico idea.*

"I have decided we should throw a surprise party for Danilo

and eat roasted pig. We can cook it in my house so that it will be a surprise. I will organise everything."

Spit-roasted barbecued pigs are the standard fare for celebrations here. I went to his house and spoke to his grandparents who said they would be delighted to help and assured me they knew exactly what to do. They told me we would need a twenty-kilo pig.

Personally, I much prefer buying my meat in plastic trays from the supermarket, without thinking too much about what happened to them before, but in this country, especially in *barrio* land it just isn't possible.

Stepson Alberto was dispatched to get the pig on Thursday from around ten miles away. On my yellow scooter. He returned with said pig, alive and strapped to the seat behind him, which had somehow grown from twenty kilos to fifty, and a letter of permission from the local mayor to confirm he had bought the pig and hadn't stolen it. Costs were already increasing as the pig was twice as big, so cost twice as much, and the letter from the mayor with his 'pig transportation permission' cost a hundred pesos. Then we had to buy a sack of charcoal, the seasoning, and various other bits and pieces. All afternoon I had people at the gate asking me what they should do, and it appeared that although I had been told they knew what to do, no one had a clue. I was beginning to think that Danilo's birthday present would be a live pig and not a party.

Anyway, I checked online and it said the pig had to be cooked for twenty-four hours so I gave strict instructions, the pit was dug, charcoal lit and the cooking began at 6pm Friday night.

All appeared to be under control as the *barrio* filled with smoke that night.

The next morning I went over to check on progress. The pig was in the kitchen. Grandmother assured me it was cooked, but I was pretty sure it wasn't. It later appeared that they had run out of charcoal and she was fed up with the smoke in her house so they just took it off the fire. More charcoal was bought and the cooking started again.

The party began at 6pm, with the invited Dominicans turning up slowly, but by 9pm the party was in full swing with everyone drinking and dancing. Shirley, my friend who I met on the Dominican Republic expat website DR1, had made the trip with Margo, her Dominican maid, and it was great to see them, and Chivirico was barman, where he was a bit too efficient as the gallon of rum disappeared in no time. In the event the pig was delicious, but there was far too much and we lived off pork for days.

As for me, I made the firm decision the next party would be cheese and pineapple on sticks.

Around the same time Chivirico and I were talking about Christmas.

"Do you know who Santa Claus is, Chivirico?" I asked him.

"Yes, of course I know," he said, "but I have never seen him as he doesn't visit naughty children and I must always have been naughty as he has never visited me nor ever given me any presents."

My heart tightened as I heard this and felt a lump come into my throat. "Well, Santa didn't visit me last year as he ran out of petrol for his sleigh, but I think he might come this year," I replied, determined to do something for this child who was wheedling his way into my heart and my life.

"What you need to do is write your list for Santa Claus, what you want for Christmas. I will help you write it, and we will burn it on the barbecue and the smoke will go all the way to the North Pole to Santa."

At this he scampered off to find a piece of paper and a pencil and the list was duly written. It had a whole range of Ben 10 things like a T-shirt, a watch, various toys, shoes and presents for his grandparents and brother and sister. He also wanted food for his family at Christmas. We went into the garden and burned the list checking that the wind was in the right direction to carry the smoke to the North Pole.

However much I wanted to make this Christmas special for him, I realised there was no way we could, as we simply did not have enough money. A Canadian friend, who had read about Chivirico in my blog, had fallen in love with him and set up his very own Facebook page so I swallowed my pride and asked anyone who wanted to help him to have a great Christmas to donate to the cause. I was overwhelmed at the response, which meant not only could we get everything on the list, there was also US$150 for his family so they could have a fabulous Christmas Eve dinner. The dinner on Christmas Eve, *Noche buena* is the most important meal of the year in the Dominican Republic. Families come from all over the country to their parents' home to be together and eat the traditional food of roast pig or chicken, rice and peas, *moro con guandules*, Russian salad – which is like potato salad with eggs, potatoes, beetroot and onion – pasta salad, ordinary salad, special Christmas bread, apples and grapes. Many families cannot pay for a meal like this, and many spend a year in debt to be able to afford it. I knew there was no way Chivirico's grandparents could afford it, as when Ana was asked about the household income at the bank when we were opening Chivirico's account, she said two thousand pesos. That is around US$50 a month.

Every day Chivirico would come running to the house to open his advent calendar. My mum had sent him an online Jacqui Lawson advent calendar and each day something happened when you clicked on the date. Chiv adored it and was totally smitten and desperate to open it each day. Once he had opened the calendar he always asked whether Santa had received his list, so I decided to try and find if there was some way Santa could communicate with him. I discovered a website which had a video from Santa – you just had to provide some information and then Santa would send a video. Unfortunately, Santa didn't have the name Chivirico in his list of names – odd that – but he did have Yuri and given his real name is Eury, I thought they sounded close enough.

Chivirico turned up as usual after lunch.

"Hey, I have a message for you from Santa here," I announced, off handedly.

"You do? You really do? A message? For me? From Santa? Really from Santa?" He jumped up and down and could hardly contain his excitement. I loaded the video and he sat watching wide-eyed and open-mouthed. The video was in English but I translated it for him, and Santa had a book with his name on and his photo and then he had to check if he had been good or naughty. Chiv held his breath when Santa said he had to check and it was a full fifteen seconds before Santa announced that Chivirico had been good. His little eyes welled up with tears, as did mine, then he cheered and ran around the room yelling, "I have been good! Santa is coming! Santa is coming!"

We had to watch the video time and time again, but the only problem was that Santa said "Hello, Yuri," and Chivirico wanted to say "Hello, Santa" back, but Santa wouldn't stop talking. We watched the video at least twice a day every day and within a week he would recite the whole thing in English as Santa spoke, but try as he might, Santa would never shut up and listen to him.

He carried on cooking every day, as there was always something he needed to raise money for and buy. This time it was a tree for his house, as they had never had one, and it had to have lights and a fairy, but within two days of yuca fritters and chocolate brownies we had enough for a small tree and lights and, of course, the fairy.

We needed to work out a way to get the money to him which had been donated to his grandmother by his Facebook fans so she could buy all that was needed for the Christmas Eve meal. We knew things were really hard as they had had no money for food at all for a few days, so I took Chivirico into our bedroom to watch television and I sent Danilo outside. He too adored Chivirico and loved what I was trying to do to give him the best Christmas ever, so he was keen to help in any way he could.

"You need to make the noise of a reindeer," I instructed Danilo.

"What is raydee?"

"It is the animal which pulls Santa's sleigh," I explained.

"Oh. A camel."

"No, it is not a bloody camel. It's like a horse with sticks on its head," I tried to explain, having no idea of the Spanish word for reindeer.

"A horse *con estick*? Okay I unnerstan. They make same noise as camel," he said knowingly.

I went into the bedroom with Chivirico and suddenly I heard this snorting sound.

"Chivirico, did you hear that noise. Sounded like a reindeer to me." He looked at me as if I was going mad. Then the noise happened again.

"**That** is definitely a reindeer," he pronounced, looking very serious and turned back to watch the television.

Suddenly, an expertly aimed envelope came flying in through the window, hit the ceiling and plopped onto the floor in front of him. His eyes grew like saucers and he picked it up. On the front it said 'Chivirico's Grandma' in Spanish. He leapt up, ran around the room and jumped up and down on the bed, before sprinting out of the door, down the path and charging down the dusty track to his grandma's house.

"*Abuela, abuela,* look! The reindeer brought this. It has your name on it, but I have to open it," he spluttered, barely able to get the words out.

His grandmother, Beatrice, stood laughing with her greying hair falling out of its bun as she wiped her hand down her flowered apron.

"Come in Lindsay, *entra,*" she laughed. "Would you like coffee?"

"*Abuela*, we have to open this now," ordered Chivirico, as he tore open the envelope revealing five RD$1,000 notes, around US$130. Beatrice stopped what she was doing as her jaw dropped. I doubt she had seen that much money in years.

"This is for Christmas dinner from Santa Claus," yelled Chivirico as he charged around the little wooden home waving the money in his hand, while I silently thanked those who had donated it.

On Christmas Eve, the family had a fabulous meal of chicken and pork, rice and peas, Russian salad, Christmas bread and pasta salad.

After dinner, Chivirico came round to my house and relieved me of my bottle of rum for Santa, luckily there wasn't much left in it, and also took a carrot to leave for the reindeer. He was so excited, I have no idea how he slept.

On Christmas morning we awoke early and went to hide Chivirico's presents in the dog crate at the back of the garden. Half munched carrots laid a trail to the crate. At seven thirty in the morning Chivirico arrived to open day twenty-five on his advent calendar, which my mum had sent. He said Santa must have been to his house as the bottle of rum was empty and the carrot had gone. He had searched but couldn't find any presents – he thought probably as he didn't have a chimney there was no way Santa could leave the presents. His only hope was he left them in our house near where the smoke from his list had gone. The search began in my house. Not one cupboard was left unchecked, and he searched under every bed ably aided by the dogs, who thought it was some sort of new game.

Eventually he spotted the carrots in the garden and discovered the presents in the dog crate, which resulted in more running around and yelling. He took the presents back to his house and we all had to come along and watch him opening each one slowly and giving the presents to the other members of his family. While he adored all of his Ben 10 items, his favourites were his chef's hat and apron with his name on it and his Winnie the Pooh cookbook.

Then Lala had a stroke. She was taken to the local clinic and from there transferred to the public hospital in Santiago, which was around an hour away. Every day I would ask her husband, Michael, and her daughter, Chivirico's stepmother, how she was. Her husband said he had spoken to the doctors who said it could go two ways. She would get better or she would get worse. I couldn't argue with that.

A week or so after that, I heard screaming and shouting from Lala's house and assumed she had died. The street was full of people scampering along to her house, and I asked Danilo to go and check what had happened. Within a few minutes he came back.

"Her brain is there, but it no work. She cannot move arms and legs. Hospital send her home to die in house. She die soon. Maybe tomorrow maybe next day."

"Does she have a nurse with her? Who will take care of her? Has she got a drip? Medicines?"

"The family help. No need for nurse or doctor. She will die soon."

It all seemed brutal to me, no pain relief, no special care. And Lala surprised them all.

I went to see her every day, three or four times a day. No way was she brain dead. Her little wooden house was always full as her myriad children returned from various parts of the country, and indeed the world, to see her. The men sat outside on the terrace, and the women sat inside in the living area. There was rarely anyone in the bedroom with Lala, unless the priest came, when they all crammed into her little bedroom to pray.

When I went into see her she was lying flat, with no pillow. She was snoring gently, her hair spread out on the pillow around her and with a feeding tube in her nose. She was dressed in the same nightie she always wore and covered with a sheet. It was stifling hot in the room, and the fan she usually had in her bedroom was keeping her children cool in the living room.

I sat next to her on the bed and squeezed her hand. She opened her eyes and seemed to focus on me, so I sat chatting to her as I usually did, telling her about Chivirico's recent exploits. I asked her to squeeze my hand if she could hear me and I swear she did. I walked back into the living room.

"Listen, I am sure Lala may recover. All you have to do is sit her up a little so her chest doesn't become congested, and sit and talk to her. Try and exercise her arms and legs as well." They looked at me as if I was a raving nutter, and went back to their conversation and I heard the words "*gringa loca*" as they muttered under their breath.

I continued to see her every day, three or four times a day, and each time she was lying flat again, and each time I asked them to sit her up and talk to her. I could tell the family were becoming restless and wanting to return to their homes – almost as if they wanted her to hurry up and die.

It was a Wednesday, around a week after Lala had returned home and I called in to see her on the way to the *colmado*. She was the same. Flat on her back again. I sat and chatted for a while, holding her hand and stroking her hair. One of her sons who had arrived said he had asked a doctor from the local private clinic to come and see her at 4pm. I went again at 2pm. Her breathing was fine, her pulse was strong, she squeezed my hand.

"I'll call in and see you later, once the doctor has been," I said to her as I walked out.

At 4.30pm I was sitting in my house working on my computer and I heard a dreadful wail, and then more and more and more. Screaming and howling. The street was full of people running to Lala's house. Lala was dead. I couldn't believe she had died, as a couple of hours earlier she had been fine.

I ran around to the house.

"What on earth happened?" I asked her son from New York. "She was fine a couple of hours ago."

"The doctor came and gave her an injection," he replied, calmly.

"What injection? What was in it?"

"*No se*. I don't know," he answered, and turned away to speak to someone else.

Dominicans, on the whole, trust doctors implicitly and never ask what medicines they are being given, nor what injections they are having. Lala's family just let the doctor inject her without knowing what it was. They said they still didn't know. Twenty minutes later she was dead.

Dominicans are brilliantly efficient at death. Within no time at all she was laid in her coffin in what used to be the living room, which was cleared of furniture, and the coffin placed atop a large block of ice to try and keep it cool on top of the dining table. All night long the family stayed up and friends and neighbours visited and consoled them. I went to see her out of respect to the family, although I really didn't want to see her body. It was fine though. What I saw lying in the coffin wasn't Lala. It was her body, yes, but she wasn't there. She had been there a few hours earlier when I had been talking to her, but she had gone. Throughout the night the sound of the crying and howling was heart-wrenching.

The following day was the funeral. We went to the local Catholic church first, and then to the cemetery. Outside the church an enterprising chap was selling ice cream out of a cooler and the *colmado* was handing out plastic bags to women for their hair as it was spitting with rain. We then set off for the three-mile walk to the cemetery through the town centre. At the front of the procession was a man holding a wooden cross, then the hearse, with the family walking next to it touching it, then people walking, then the motorcycles and finally the cars. The spitting stopped and the sun came out, beating down on us as we walked slowly.

The procession seemed to go on forever. People were singing hymns and crying, and the men kept leaving the procession to have a pee behind trees. A couple of hours later we reached the cemetery on the far side of town and the coffin was unloaded and carried through the higgledy-piggledy graveyard to the crypt.

People were climbing on top of the different crypts to get a good view, like playing in a kids' playground -- somewhat ghoulish 1 thought, but that is the custom, 1 suppose. The screaming then became hysterical, with some of her children having to be restrained from climbing into the crypt alongside the coffin. Their grief was almost unbearable to watch and a couple of the women even screamed themselves into unconsciousness and had to be carried away.

Lala was mourned for nine days, with a mass every day at 4pm in the house and on the ninth day there was the final farewell, another mass, food for everyone, and then the furniture went back inside, and her husband Michael, also in his eighties, started his life alone.

1 will always wonder what was in that injection. Danilo told me it often happened when the family came from *Nuevo Yol* and only had a couple of days holiday, that if the parent did not die as quickly as expected, they did not believe in prolonging their holiday as they had to get back for work. Therefore the parent was 'put to sleep'. 1 was to learn more about this practice as the years passed.

RIP Lala.

CHAPTER THREE
WASP HOUSE

*"And whether or not it is clear to you, no doubt
the universe is unfolding as it should."*
Desiderata, Max Ehrmann 1927

I WAS WORKING AS USUAL, SITTING AT THE LAPTOP, WHICH WAS on a coffee table along with a half-filled ashtray and a bottle of water, swatting the incessant mosquitoes and flies buzzing around. Chivirico was in the kitchen end of the kitchen diner making brownies, standing on a chair so he could reach the kitchen work surface, with his chef's hat perched on his head and his apron covered in brownie batter.

"Americana!" was shouted outside from what sounded like a young child. *"Americana!"*

"*Voy.*" I am coming, yelled Chiv as he scrambled down from his perch with wooden spoon in hand dripping batter all over the floor. He ran out of the door and reappeared a minute or so later.

"It is two Haitian girls. They are very poor. They have no father and their mother has gone to *La Capital* to work. They are hungry and have no money and want to wash your clothes for money. So, I gave them your dirty clothes. They will be back with your clothes all clean by five o'clock."

"You did what? You gave them my clothes?" I asked incredulously, thinking I would never see my clothes again.

"They need the money and your clothes were dirty," he announced, as he sauntered back to the kitchen. "Anyway, you hate washing and you aren't very good at it either," he added with his cheeky grin.

I shook my head in resignation and went back to work.

Five o'clock arrived and no sign of the Haitian girls nor my clothes. Chivirico was becoming concerned and I vaguely heard him saying, "Okay, I will go and fetch your clothes on my bicycle."

"Hmm, yeah whatever," I answered distractedly, not really listening to him and once again went back to work. A while later, as the number of mosquitoes increased, I realised it was becoming dusk and there was no sign of Chivirico, no sign of the Haitian girls and no sign of my clothes. He had been gone hours and I also realised I had no idea where these girls lived. As the sun began to disappear I thought I had better let his grandmother know I didn't know where he was. Very bad move on my part.

I picked my way across the potholed and rubbish strewn street and walked the hundred yards down the street to her little wooden house.

"*Hola*, Lindsay. Where is Eury?" she asked, smiling at me.

"Well, that's the *problemita*," I answered. "He went to look for my washing," and I explained what had happened.

"But I'm sure he'll be back soon," I ended confidently.

"Those girls live a very long way away, on the other side of the canal. I will have to tell his father."

I gulped, knowing Chiv would not get away with this lightly.

"Well, please tell him it is not Eury's fault. It is mine. And please, please tell him not to hit him. Please," I begged.

I went home, hoping Chiv would have arrived, but there was still no sign of him and the next thing I saw was a furious-looking Chiv's dad zooming past the house on his motorbike.

All I could do was pray and when Danilo arrived back I sighed with relief as if there was one person who could sort this out it was him.

"*Gracias a Dios* you're home!" I rapidly explained what had happened.

It was only around ten minutes later that two tearful Haitian girls turned up at the gate. They held my scrunched up clothes in their arms, were puffing and panting and shaking with fear.

Thank goodness, I thought. *Chivirico can't be far behind them.*

"Sorry, *Americana*," the older one stammered, trying to get the words out. "He came and they were clean, your clothes were lovely and clean." The smaller one interrupted, "And they were ironed and all nice in a bag."

"Yes, and ironed and Chivirico's dad saw us and he threw them on the ground and now they are dirty and he pulled Eury off his bike and he was kicking him in the dirt on the ground."

"He is kicking him and hitting him with his belt, and Eury is screaming."

"And we ran here so you can help him and sorry about your clothes, but he is kicking him in the street – you have to help him," and they grabbed my arm and tried to pull me out of the gate.

I had to fight to stop myself from vomiting there and then as the fury mounted in me and I was running out of the gate when Danilo ran outside and grabbed my arm firmly above the elbow and pulled me back in.

"No. This is family. You are not family. A father can do what he likes to his children to discipline them and it is not your place to interfere."

"But it's my fault!" I wailed, as I fought to get free. "Chiv was only trying to help. Please, help me – he has to stop hitting him, he has to."

At that moment we heard the motorbike approaching. Chivirico's dad was riding it, with Chiv behind him on the seat, covered in mud and crying, with his father dragging Chiv's bicycle along by the other hand.

"Danilo, I have to go and see if he is okay," I begged.

"No. This is a family matter, it is not your place to interfere," he ordered, and held me tightly in his arms as I sobbed. *What the hell were they doing to that little boy?*

I slumped on the sofa with my head in my hands, thinking how much this amazing tiny little boy, who had so much joy inside him, was suffering and how much he was hurting. Then I heard the gate open and Chiv rushed into the room and into my arms sobbing his little heart out, gasping for breath.

He was covered in mud and his little face was filthy with tracks made by his falling tears.

"I am sorry, Lindsay. I didn't know it was so far."

"Chiv don't be silly, it isn't your fault. It's mine. And I told him not to hit you. I begged him. Oh, come here and let's have a big cuddle." He clambered onto my lap and held me tightly, sobbing into my shoulder, but within a few minutes the sobbing subsided and we went and washed his face and I put him in the shower to clean him off. As I gently washed him down with a facecloth, looking at his beautiful smooth back and stomach now covered with angry welts I swear I had never felt such total and overwhelming fury in my life. There was absolutely nothing I could do, but I knew Danilo was right, Chivirico was not my child, but how dare his father do that to this gorgeous child who was only trying to help. How could anyone hit their own child like that?

Danilo went to speak to his father who assured him he hadn't kicked him – he had just used his belt – the buckle end.

In *barrio* land the universe was unfolding as only it can and a whole range of things were happening and coming together, which would lead to the next stage of our lives.

On the financial side life was still not easy as the new UK pension regulations meant my pension went down month by month and we continued to live on the breadline. And every month the pension decreased as some UK government expert assumed we would live longer. The main issues were that every month half of my pension went on paying back a bank loan, which the bank had refused to reschedule, and half of the remainder went on rent. Danilo was still at university and loving it and doing well, but he was becoming more and more frustrated with *barrio* life as was I. The lack of electricity, the swarms of mosquitoes and flies along with the general unsanitary living conditions were not conducive to studying or working.

I had, unbelievably, found a publisher for my book, *What About Your Saucepans?* and was busy working with her, along with the editor, the proof reader and the designer to get it ready for printing. Being an optimistic sort of person I imagined there was a chance the book would make us lots of money and as I lay in bed at night listening to the whirr of the fan, the cocks crowing and the mosquitoes with their high pitched whines, my mind drifted to the Oscars, where I was walking down the red carpet and watching as the film of the book took the Oscar for best film, or best screenplay or best something.

I was working writing articles for expat magazines and websites, most of which didn't pay, but I hoped the exposure would pay off and it was a way of marketing the book when it was published. I was also working for a British man, Jonathan, who had an online law firm and who employed me to market his company so that was bringing in much needed cash, which slowly increased as the months went on.

Plus, Danilo and I began to work together to help expat women who were having issues with their Dominican men.

It started innocently enough.

A Canadian lady, we will call her Cathy – who I had never met, but we had a mutual acquaintance – was married to a Dominican in jail for supposed drug dealing. He swore he had not done it. She had no idea what to do and as she was working back in Canada she asked us for help. She had appointed a lawyer in Puerto Plata, on the north coast, who happily took a great deal of money but did nothing at all to help her. Danilo was very excited as it meant he could be a real live lawyer and he sprung into action.

Over the next ten months or so, Danilo made frequent trips to Puerto Plata, visited the guy who was on remand in jail, talked to lawyers, judges and prosecutors and when the trial took place after the guy had been on remand for twelve months, he was found not guilty and released. Danilo was super proud of himself and Cathy was very grateful.

I began to receive more and more messages from women who wanted help or advice about their relationships with Dominican men and one of these was Lynne (not her real name). Lynne messaged me on Facebook wanting to send money for Christmas for Chivirico and she bought him his beloved chef's hat and apron. She told me she was going to marry a Dominican called Pedro the following August and invited me, Danilo and Chivirico to the wedding in Jarabacoa. We chatted most days and when she couldn't get hold of Pedro she would confide in me and we even spoke to him as he had told her he was having problems in getting hold of his birth certificate for the wedding, so Danilo offered to help.

We didn't want to stay in the *barrio*, we seemed to have a potential for income from women with issues with Dominican men, plus the book would be published soon and I had more income coming in from Jonathan. And then I had a letter from my financial adviser saying there might be a way to cash my pension in. The die was cast.

We both had this dream of living on a little farm in the mountains and going to the land we had in Barahona, where Danilo was born, but this was really not an option as it was still more or less inaccessible. Danilo came from Barahona and we had bought land on the top of the mountain with no water, no electricity, no nothing but an amazing view. Getting there was almost impossible with a seven-mile trek up the hills on a road where a four-wheel drive was imperative.

When my pension was cashed we would have enough to pay off the bank loan and to buy somewhere small and basic with a little bit of land. Both being foolish romantics, we thought that if we didn't have enough money to live on we could grow our own food so at least we wouldn't be hungry. We also needed to be within commutable distance of the university – preferably with public transport as Danilo was having problems driving my Jeep – he still had no idea how to change gear, could only do first to second. Those of you who have read *What about Your Saucepans?* will remember how I often do things without thinking of the consequences or logically looking at all the ramifications, but something in my head was loving the idea of the simple life. I remembered my mother telling me the happiest time of her life was when the four of her children were all under six and we lived in a caravan with gas lamps, tiny fridge and no mod cons. That had always stuck in my head.

"So, Danilo, where are we going to look?" I asked, one Saturday morning.

"I have a friend at university who lives in the mountains, let's go and see him and see what he says," he replied excitedly. There is nothing Danilo does better than get involved in new projects and spend money.

So off we set in the Jeep driving through the *barrio* to the local town of Mao and then up into the mountains towards a mountain town high up to the north of *Pico Duarte*, the highest mountain in the Caribbean. The town was called Monción and was home to an enormous dam with stupendous views. As we drove higher and higher I could not help but feel my heart soar – it reminded me of going to visit my grandmother in Wales.

On the mountain road some eleven kilometres before Monción, we arrived in the small *campo* where Danilo's friend Christian lived, called Cacique, which means Taíno Indian chief. Cacique had around four hundred inhabitants and there were houses either side of the road and dirt tracks going off each side of the road with more houses. The houses were a combination of brightly coloured wooden huts with zinc roofs, and houses built of concrete. All were beautifully kept, fenced in with brilliantly vibrant bougainvillea and hibiscus flowers along the fences.

We met Christian at a local restaurant where he worked. This was the only restaurant in the area and there was no need for a menu as it only sold stewed goat. In fact, it was so famous for its goat that at the weekend it would be crammed full, with people coming from miles around to eat there. He promised to let us know if there was anything for sale and confirmed there was public transport to the university, although the buses only went every hour. He told us there was electricity twenty-four hours a day, although it did sometimes go off for a few hours on a Friday and that there was no issue with the water supply. This all sounded very positive, especially the electricity, and so Danilo began a serious hunt. For the next few Saturdays we descended on the *campo* to look at what he had found.

The first house was a typical Dominican summer home made of wood with a zinc roof, but there was no kitchen (most people cook outside on a *fogon*, which is an outdoor cooking stove with wood for fuel), the rooms were very small and although the garden was full of avocado and mango trees and all sorts of fruit and vegetables, there was no mountain view and it was quite a long walk from the road if you needed to catch the bus.

We kept looking, but could find nothing and then Danilo decided it would be better to build a house. I wasn't too happy with that idea as I knew he would run dramatically over budget and we would end up with half a house and no money. In the event, luckily, we couldn't find the right piece of land to buy.

On one of our house-hunting trips Danilo arranged for us to meet a lawyer, who was supposedly selling a house for someone. We met him in the car park outside the village shop, opposite the goat restaurant, and he turned up on the back of a motorbike in his creased suit, with his file of papers in a brown cardboard folder, as his car had run out of petrol – typical lawyer. We followed the motorbike back down the hill through the village and turned right into a little track and then right again into a track – which was so overgrown we could not keep driving.

"Danilo, are you sure about this?" I asked, carefully picking my way through the two-foot high grass and weeds.

"We see," he answered, as we came to what should be a large imposing gateway – if it had had a gate. We walked through and I gasped. There to the left of the gate was a massive white concrete building. It appeared to be built upstairs with a wrap around balcony and balustrades but an open downstairs – almost like a multistorey car park. There was a very large overgrown area to the front of the house and we struggled to walk through that and through the hole where the front door should have been.

The floor in the car park, as I called it, was tiled with what looked like nice tiles, but covered in dirt. The house was open all the way around with what looked like a large area of completely overgrown land behind and the odd palm tree visible sticking up above the weeds and grass. There was a fully fitted downstairs bathroom; another room, a room which was tiled and ready to fit a kitchen and what looked like a dining room. There were some doors and where there were windows they were proper sliding glass windows. It was massive. Now it was time to go upstairs, but the stairway was covered with wasps' nests.

"Nope. No way am I going upstairs. I don't want to be stung," I protested.

"These are nice wapses," pronounced Danilo. "They are friendly, they don't esting."

"No, they are non estinging wasps," agreed the lawyer, nodding knowledgably as we made our way upstairs – again the stairs were nicely tiled although there was no banister. I was terrified walking up the stair past the massive wasps' nests, but the wapses just looked at me and not one stung me or even came near. Definitely nice wapses.

Upstairs was fully fitted out, only all of the interior doors were missing. There was a large living area, three bedrooms, one with its own balcony and the view of the mountains and the valley below was to die for. The house was actually at thirteen hundred feet so it was much cooler than lower down, and it came with ten *tareas* of land, which was already fenced with barbed wire and wooden posts, although very overgrown. A *tarea* is 0.155 of an acre so that made it around one-and-a-half acres. It seemed like a very big garden to me.

The lawyer explained that the house was owned by two Dominican brothers, one of whom lived in New York, and they had built it as a billiard hall – hence the open space which was originally for four billiard tables downstairs. The plan was that they would live upstairs, but with the recession in the US they ran out of money to keep building it and so it was for sale and they were open to offers. It took us no time at all to make the offer, which was accepted, and as Danilo had called me *Doña*, or 'Ma'am', during the negotiation process they did not know we were related and so he was also paid his commission as is the Dominican tradition for anyone who introduces someone to buy a house, or use a lawyer, plumber, carpenter whatever.

And of course Danilo paid me half.

We had found the house and all we had to do was wait for the pension money to arrive into my English bank account and then transfer it to my Dominican bank account. That should be simple I thought, but knowing all transactions over US$10,000 required proof of where the money was coming from, I went into the Banco Popular where we lived and I told them I would be transferring money from England and gave them the paperwork. They checked my account and told me the account was held at the branch where I used to live, in Juan Dolio, so I needed to tell that branch. I asked them to transfer my account to their branch. Apparently they couldn't do that. I had to telephone my old branch myself, which I did. Unfortunately, the only way you could transfer your account to another branch was to physically go to your old branch, at the other end of the country, some five or six hours away, and tell them personally. It could not be done by phone, fax or email. As I needed the money quickly I told them I would just go and open an account in another bank in the town, which didn't seem to bother them at all.

So off I trotted over the road to Banreservas, which is the main bank owned by the State and walked up to customer services and said I wanted to open an account.

"No problem," said the nice lady, and we started filling in the forms. Which is when the problems started.

"Do you want an account in dollars or pesos?" she asked.

"Dollars," I replied.

"Fine," she said, and I thought I had better ask what seemed like a stupid question.

"Can I take the dollars out of the account?"

"No," she said. "You can have an account in dollars, but at the moment we are not letting people take money out of them, well, maybe a little, but not very much."

"Let me get this right," I said. "I can transfer money from England into a dollar account here, but once it is here I can't take it out?"

"Correct," she replied with a smile. "We need the dollars as the country does not have many of them at the moment."

"My dollars?"

"*Exactamente.*"

"Well, I don't think I want a dollar account then," I said, as it seem a little pointless to have money in a bank which you are not allowed to touch. So I decided to open an account in Dominican pesos, where you were allowed to take the money out.

Off we started with the forms. She asked for my ID card, called a *cedula*, and for my passport. Technical hitch number two. The names are different. My *cedula* had my old married name and my passport my new married name. She decided I couldn't open an account with my *cedula*, I would have to use my passport.

"Is that a problem?" I asked.

"Not at all," she said. An hour passed and eventually all the paperwork was done and I was passed to another person to upload the information onto the computer system. Lady number two looked at my passport, which says on the front, 'United Kingdom of Great Britain and Northern Ireland', and inside it says I am a British citizen.

"What nationality are you?" she asked.

"English," I replied.

This was far too much for her. Understandably I suppose, she couldn't get her head around people from the United Kingdom being British citizens, had never heard of the United Kingdom nor Great Britain and what was worse couldn't find either country, United Kingdom nor Great Britain, in her list of countries on the computer. I suggested looking for England, but she insisted on going through the whole list. By this time I was sitting next to her behind the desk as we slowly went through the list.

"Hooray, I have found it," she said. "Barbados says United Kingdom next to it in brackets. You must be from Barbados."

I assured her I wasn't. Portugal maybe, she said, Peru, British Virgin Isles? It took at least fifteen minutes and eventually she discovered England, which, she said she had also never heard of, and had major doubts that the United Kingdom and England were one and the same place, and I was a British citizen according to my passport so probably came from neither of them.

The interview continued. "What is your occupation?"

"Writer," I said proudly. No occupation of writer listed in the computer.

"Could you be something else?" she enquired.

"What would you like me to be?" I asked politely.

"How about an architect?" she said. I suggested a plumber and she said I couldn't be that as I was a woman. In the end we settled on journalist.

Finally, all the data was in the computer and I received my little book with my opening balance of 500 pesos in it.

"Where is my card so I can get money out of the ATM?" I asked.

"You can't take money out of this account yet," she said.

"Err why not?" I asked. "I will be transferring money from England and will need to get the money out of the account as soon as it arrives here."

"Well, you can't," she announced. "The account is frozen, because you used your passport to open it. Your passport needs to be verified."

"How long will that take?"

"Around a month. Maybe a little longer."

"Is that a Dominican month?" I enquired, knowing it could be a lot longer.

In the end, my original bank discovered that they could take the fund transfer and after three years I had a call from BanReservas saying that my ATM card was now ready.

Chivirico was not a happy bunny and I must admit I was pretty upset about leaving him too.

"I won't see you when you move. You will forget about me," he mumbled tearfully.

"I could never forget about you, silly boy. This is not just our house, it will be your house too, so let's go and have a look at it and you can decide which will be your bedroom. You can come at weekends and in the school holidays. Okay?" That seemed to placate him and the next weekend we set off for 'Wasp House' as it was now called.

It looked no better on the second visit, and there was so much to be done. Danilo wandered around looking at things and thinking.

"Lindsay, you won't see this again like this. I will sort everything. The next time you see Wapse house, she will be finish," he announced.

Chivirico decided which room would be his bedroom and said he wanted bunk beds so he could have room for visitors and his earlier concerns seemed to disappear.

We also had to sort out Dany and Alberto. Neither wanted to move with us, as there was nothing to do in the *campo* and neither had a job. The problem was that as long as they lived with us they had a roof over their heads and food, so getting a job was not high on the list of priorities. I agreed to pay three months deposit for a new home for them, a wooden hut but with an inside bathroom – rather than a latrine in the yard – and to let them have half of our furniture including the stove, fridge, fan, two beds and a sofa, and to give them enough money to live on for two months. After that, they were on their own and had to find work. As it was it took them a week to find jobs in the Free Zone, a place where sweat shop labour was used sewing clothes for American clothing companies at a pittance of a wage, around US$150 a month. But at least they had jobs.

Once the paperwork was signed and the money handed over in mid-January 2013, Danilo more or less moved in to camp at Wasp House and began the work of sorting out the water, electricity and sewage, getting rid of the wasps, the Haitian who was squatting upstairs, and putting in walls, doors and a kitchen. He had in his mind the date of 28th February to move in as that was my father's birthday. Everything was happening at the same time – moving into the new house and the book being published, I felt overwhelmed with excitement.

The usual house-moving plan would then take place, which involved me going to a hotel for a couple of nights while Danilo moved the animals and furniture to save me being stressed. He would design the kitchen, decide on the layout of downstairs, where the walls would go and the whole colour scheme.

While he was busy at Wasp House, I was busy getting the book ready for publishing, which happened so quickly it was amazing. The design was done, just the final touches and then it was ready to go. Looking for the publisher for the book, *What About Your Saucepans?* had been a long and arduous process. I sent around a hundred emails to publishers and agents with an excerpt from the book and a summary of what it was about and most replied saying that whilst the manuscript was intriguing it was "not right for our list". I was never sure if the manuscript was rubbish and they were being nice, in a very Dominican way, telling me what they thought I wanted to hear, or if they were telling the truth. Some would say it needed editing and would send me to an editor who would charge to edit it, which meant less food that month and then I would resubmit and they would say the same, "not right for our list".

In the end one publisher, Jo Parfitt, of Summertime Publishing, gave me a glimmer of hope and said if I changed all sorts of things, like introduced dialogue, described the characters in much more detail, and "showed what happened, rather than tell," she would look at it. That is when I started to learn how to write. She put me in touch with an amazing editor, Jane Dean, and little by little I started to rewrite it. It was very hard writing dialogue, and it was even harder digging deep into my memory and my soul and writing about my feelings and all the things that had happened over the previous ten years or so, many of which I would rather forget. Jo also told me to start a blog and if I could get three thousand visitors a month to the blog and made the changes she asked for, and worked with Jane, then she would publish the book. It seemed like a tall order, but I set up the blog and had three visits for the first post, one of which was my mum and two were me. But I kept going and within six months I had the three thousand required visitors and off we went with the final changes.

At the same time a friend of mine who bred Siberian Huskies asked me if I wanted one, so of course I said "yes", but did no research into the breed. Chivirico came with us to pick him up and fell in love immediately with this tiny, furry, white teddy bear. Lobo, meaning wolf in Spanish, arrived to join Meg, Silly Boy and Belinda. He looked beautiful, white with green eyes, but we soon found out that Lobos would chase cats, eat chickens and if allowed to would run for miles – and not come back. Luckily, at the pink house he could not get out, but Danilo knew we would have to have a way of stopping him from escaping at Wasp House and all of the neighbours had chickens which wandered freely onto our land, so there would be trouble ahead.

The 27th February arrived, which is a key day for the Dominican Republic. It is the date when the country became an independent nation from Haiti in 1844. It was even more important as that was the date *What About Your Saucepans?* was published.

I was eagerly waiting for copies of my book to arrive from England as I wanted to hold a book launch here, but it was prohibitively expensive to post them and even more of a risk that they might not arrive at all, so luckily for me Jonathan offered to bring them back with him as he was returning from a trip to the UK. He purchased a new suitcase for the purpose and also included the thing I miss most from the UK – parsnips. As soon as he landed on Dominican soil he sent one of his Dominican employees to the bus company, Caribe Tours, and put the suitcase on the bus to me. We use buses as the postal service here. The employee called me to tell me when it would arrive.

I eagerly went to the local office of the bus company and there was said suitcase. I could hardly contain my excitement and was desperate to open it. But the suitcase was padlocked with a small, but good quality, Globe padlock.

"Err, this suitcase has a padlock on it," I said, through the smeared glass window.

"Of course," the yellow shirted Caribe lady replied. "Did you want what was in it to be stolen?"

"Well, of course not, but I need to open it. Is there a package for me with the key in it?"

"No," she replied brusquely, but when Danilo, who was waiting outside in the car, saw it he said, "No worry I esnap it off."

I called Jonathan who said he hadn't put the padlock on, but the bus company did and gave the key to his Dominican employee who had taken the case to the bus. He had the key in his pocket and when Jonathan asked him about it the employee said he knew Danilo would know how to esnap the padlock off, as all Dominicans knew that.

So why did the bus company employees not esnap the bloody padlock off? I asked myself.

Why not use a tie wrap, which costs a fraction of the price and is easier to get off? The lock wouldn't actually snap off, it had to be sawn off. And there inside were my books. And parsnips. Bliss.

We were ready to move and it was time for me to leave for the hotel. I waved goodbye to the cats and dogs and the pink house, gave Chivirico a massive hug and promised I would see him soon and set off, surprisingly tearful, in my Jeep for two nights at the hotel in Mao, while Danilo sorted everything. He had been constantly at Wasp House for six weeks and I had rarely seen him, although I had heard mutterings about interior designers (you are kidding me) and landscapers and granite work tops, but I had only given him US$10,000 to do everything – including fitting the kitchen out, putting in walls, windows, doors and gates, painting and decorating, fumigating the wasps – nice or not – curtains, and clearing the land.

The hotel was bliss. Great food, air conditioning, no mosquitoes, but I was ready to see the new house. The 28th February came and went, as did 1st and 2nd March. I kept calling Danilo.

"Okay. Is it ready? Can I come today?"

"No, is no ready. Still thing to do. You come tomorrow. Maybe. Maybe not tomorrow maybe next day," he would reply.

I had a phone call from Ana, Chivirico's aunt, saying he was inconsolable as I hadn't called him to visit and I felt dreadful, but explained I wasn't there yet. At last, on 3rd March, Danilo called me and said I could come to Wapse House. It was ready.

Many people ask me how I could not be involved in the design of the new house. We were not just changing the curtains – there were walls to be put in, a whole kitchen to be fitted, windows, doors to be fitted. To be honest I knew Danilo adored making my life easy, and adored giving me surprises. At the end of the day it was just a house, it didn't really matter to me what colour the walls were, or even where the walls were. I was happy to let him have the pleasure of designing and planning it, and dreaming about how I would react when I saw it. He got pleasure giving me pleasure and I got pleasure knowing he was getting pleasure doing it. Two-way street.

I packed my bag quickly, rushed down to reception, checked out and threw my bag in the Jeep ready to go to my new – this time, forever – home. The road that winds up to the mountains was good and the views got better and better and the air fresher and cooler as I turned off the main road onto the road to the village, which became so steep I had to drive the last part in first gear. I turned left onto the track, and then right onto the other one, and the first thing I noticed was that where there had previously been a gap for a gate, there was now a big solid metal gate which Hector rolled back so I could drive in.

Hector, you may remember, was some relation of Danilo's from Bani in the south of the country, and had been shot in the leg by the police when working with us on the mayoral campaign. He was the person who accused me of trying to poison him by giving him pork chops when he had been shot – when everyone knows if you eat pork when injured you die. The rule obviously doesn't apply to pork sausages as he had those instead with no ill effects. Hector had been living in Wasp House to keep an eye on it since we bought it and he had been helping with the renovations. There were neighbours peering over the back fence and all waving at me, like some sort of welcoming committee and I could already feel a lump in my throat as the tears threatened. I was coming home at last and maybe this would be my forever home.

Where the hole for the front door had been was a massive metal double door, like something from a stately home, and where part of the multistorey car park had been was a doghouse with all the dogs barking excitedly at me. Danilo stood at the door.

"Welcome to your Wapse House, my love," he said, grinning like the Cheshire Cat. I walked inside and gasped. The whole back wall was glass patio doors all the way across. The view was stunning and the room looked enormous. It was painted in a sand-coloured yellow that looked perfect, with floaty Turkish brothel curtains on all the windows in deep orange, green and yellow, with fronds on them and beads on the bottom. I walked through the lounge and dining area, spotting my rattan furniture which had all been recovered and restored, and went to see the kitchen. I just stood there in amazement, my arms limp by my side.

"I wanted *Americana* kitchen for you," said Danilo proudly. "Look, the microway she is on the wall. That is what *Americana* does." The whole kitchen was in mahogany, with black granite work surfaces, a built-in microwave, large cooker, and, the saints be praised, a massive fridge. At last I would have a fridge again after three years with just a tiny excuse of a fridge, which hardly worked, and I couldn't stop myself running to give it a hug. There was even an extractor fan above the cooker.

In what was supposed to be the dining room, but was now the utility room, there was a new washing machine, albeit still a Dominican twin tub, and a small chest freezer and when we went upstairs everything was equally perfect. The floaty curtains were throughout the living area and there were new covers on the beds in the guest room and our room, with curtains to match. The bathroom had matching towels, toilet seat and cistern and shower curtains. Very interior designed. It was just amazingly gorgeous, looked like a show house and I simply could not believe it, standing there with my mouth open.

Outside, what had been a jungle, had been cleared and the space nearest the house was full of beautiful flowers and palm trees. I had asked for a vegetable patch too and was expecting one like in England, a sort of square or rectangular area with different seeds planted in rows, each seed four inches apart, with the seed packet on a little stick at the end. I didn't quite have that. I had palm trees with seeds scattered around the bases. Cauliflower, carrots, peppers, chillies and my favourite parsnips with the seed packets stuck in the trees. Some had even started growing.

I spent the next few days unpacking and trying to sort things out. All of the cats had arrived safe and sound apart from Cojo the three-pawed cat. He had been born in Juan Dolio with only three paws, but managed to hop around. A reward was offered at our old house for anyone who could find him and eventually, after a couple of months, he was delivered after the reward was trebled. The cats were in their element as Danilo had made cat holes in the lovely mahogany doors and the wall in the utility room, so they could come and go at will and they could explore our land and the mahogany wood next door to their hearts' content.

The neighbours came in a constant stream. It was cold, colder than I had ever known in the Dominican Republic. By cold I mean down to 50° Fahrenheit at night and in the early morning. All of the neighbours were wearing woolly knitted hats – it was like a hoard of Compos from the BBCs *Last of the Summer Wine*. I thought I would never remember all the names and they brought food constantly. In fact, I didn't cook for the first month we were in the house as one or the other would yell to say that lunch was ready. We ate most of the time at Barbara's house, which was on the main road to the right of our house, but only about twenty yards away.

Barbara, in her late forties, was always laughing and always busy. She seemed to cook every day for anyone who was around and she cooked on her *fogon*. Not only was it cheaper as it used wood, of which there was plenty, but it also gave the food a lovely smoky taste. Her house was brightly painted and wooden, where she lived with her husband Miguel and two children, a boy and a girl, who were in their late teens and early twenties. She had a lovely garden full of fruit trees, avocados, mango, bitter oranges, papaya and a hot chilli pepper bush, which was fabulous for me as I could have fresh chillies for cooking curries and Thai food. Everyone had a gap or a gate in the fences which surrounded the gardens, so people just walked through each others' gardens and if you wanted an avocado, or mango or orange or lime, you just went and helped yourself. Occasionally there would be bartering going on, and as our garden was full of pea bushes people would come laden with yuca and plantains for us and leave with a bag full of peas. The village centre was around a mile or so up the road but we had a *colmado* close by with the basics, and a little mini bus went past every hour to Mao or Monción where there were proper shops and a halfway decent supermarket in Mao. There were, however, no *motoconcho* taxis and no normal taxis, so if you had no car, apart from the hourly bus service, which finished at 5pm, you were more or less stuck. It didn't bother me at the time.

Danilo was in his element as he loved the mountains and living off the land and when he wasn't at university he was busy visiting neighbours or pottering in the garden. Conversations continued to be as they always had been. I would call him to find out what he was up to and when he would be coming home.

Me. "Hi, where are you?"

Him."*Aqui*." Here

Me. "Where exactly is here?"

Him. "*Aqui abajo*." Here further down.

Me. "What are you doing there?"

Him."*Nada*." Nothing.

Me. "So, why are you there doing nothing?"

Him."*Hablando*." Talking.

Me. "Who are you talking to?"

Him."*Hablando disparate*." Talking rubbish.

Me. "Who are you talking rubbish with?"

Him."*Nadie*." No one.

Me. "When are you coming home?"

Him."*Ahorita*." Later

Me. "Just so I get this right. You are there, wherever there is, talking rubbish with no one and will be back later."

Him."*Exactamente*."

And I would howl with laughter. I had learned over time that there were things that it was worth being concerned about, and others which were not. What time he would be home, if we had nowhere to go to, was not one of them.

As we spent more time in the house, we discovered certain things weren't working too well, such as the downstairs toilet, which was blocked. We tried everything to unblock it, but to no avail, so Danilo dug up the garden and discovered the pipe from the toilet just stopped in the middle of the front garden and did not go all the way to the septic tank. The pipe to the septic tank was around two feet away from the toilet pipe and both were just in dirt.

"Danilo, let's just buy another piece of pipe and stick the two together," I suggested, calling on my vast plumbing experience.

"No, that won't work. The poo has to bounce off the wall," he explained. "We need to concrete the wall and bottom so the poo bouncy, and he go in other peep." And off he went to buy a bag of cement. He returned shortly afterwards with the cement and mixed up the concrete then lined the hole. In the meantime I checked bouncy poo systems on Google and it appeared he was right.

"Tomorrow we check that poo he bouncy," he announced. How could I sleep? The excitement of playing poo sticks was too much.

The following day we prepared to test the system. First we needed someone to poo in the toilet, but neither of us wanted to go, and personally I think that one's own poo is a tad private and not sure I wanted to be the one whose poo failed the bouncy test. Given Danilo appeared to be of a like mind, we used a piece of freshly made dog shit. Danilo explained that once we flushed the toilet, the poo would come charging down the pipe from the toilet, bounce off the concrete opposite the end of the pipe, like a billiard ball off the side cushion and head straight down the other pipe into the septic tank.

I was in charge of finding the dog shit, putting it in the toilet and then flushing, which I did, before scampering outside to see what was happening. The dog shit shot down the pipe, then it hit the wall, but did not bounce into the other pipe, it broke up and sat there in the hole. However, Danilo announced the test run was a success and that dog shit was not like human poo as the latter would not break up, and he put a concrete lid on the hole. The toilet has never blocked up since.

This was the first time Danilo and I had lived together alone, apart from Hector who arrived to look after the house before we moved in and just stayed. Before, the kids had always been there. There was no pressure of children and the two of us had a ball. We worked together, me on my computer and him studying. We fixed things around the house together, we gardened together, cooked together, cleaned together and laughed constantly. I had, quite simply, never been happier in my life.

CHAPTER FOUR
THREE'S A CROWD

"Be cheerful. Strive to be happy."
Desiderata, Max Ehrmann 1927

BY NOW I HAD BEEN TALKING TO THE AMERICAN LADY, LYNNE, for a few months, she who was engaged to Pedro, and they were due to marry in August 2013. She would message me on Facebook most days to ask about what she needed to get married, or if she was concerned when she could not get hold of him, as they used to talk daily. He was not a young Dominican, being in his late thirties, somewhat portly, and worked as a waiter in a hotel in Punta Cana. Lynne, who was in her early forties, had been with him for around three

years and on 17th July 2012, planned to fly to the Dominican
Republic with her grown up sons to meet him and his family.
The flights were booked, but Pedro asked her to change the
dates as he had to go and train people at another hotel in a
different part of the country. She was unable to change her
dates, but thought not being with him for few days would be
fine. In the event, his family didn't show up either until 18th
July and eventually Pedro arrived on 22nd July.

The trip was important to Lynne, as although they had
discussed marriage it was vital for her that her children met
him first. Following the trip the wedding date was set for 3rd
August 2013, to be held in the middle of the country in the
mountainous area of Jarabacoa, in a villa which would sleep
sixteen people. Lynne went ahead and booked the flights for
her and other members of her family and carried on excitedly
planning the wedding.

When she started speaking to me, it was usually the same
conversation on Facebook.

Lynne: Hi Lindsay. I can't get hold of him again;
it has been two weeks now.

Me: Maybe he has Internet issues, or electricity
issues, or has a problem with his phone?

Well, he shouldn't have electricity or Internet
issues as he is at the hotel.

No idea then. It can't be bad news or you would
have heard by now. Try not to worry.

A few days later she was back online.

> Hi. At last I have heard from him. He said he had lost his phone and had to wait till he was paid to get a new one.

> Thank goodness for that. At least you have the explanation now.

A few weeks later it was the same and she couldn't get hold of him and we had the same conversation and eventually she came back.

> I have managed to get hold of him. I rang his sister and she said he had been in a car accident and broke his phone. But he is all right, not hurt. I am a bit worried though as he said that he was having problems getting his papers, so we can't get married until August next year, 2014, and not this year.

> That is stupid. He only needs his identity card, a *cedula*, and his birth certificate and you can get both easily.

> He says there was a fire at his house, and I know that is true, and his papers were burned.

> Maybe his birth cert but he would have had his *cedula* on him, and all he needs is the *cedula* number to get a new one, and everyone knows their number off by heart.

> Can you call him and ask what the issue is?

> Sure, no worries.

I spoke to Pedro on the phone and he said he knew what he needed to get, then I put him on to Danilo.

"This man not good man," pronounced Danilo. "This bad man, he no marry Lynne." On that cheerful note I decided to investigate further.

I knew a Dominican friend, Maria, who worked at the Civil Registry and I could give her someone's details and she could find out the information about their birth, plus other information such as their children and whether they were married or divorced. Lynne gave me Pedro's name and where he was born, along with the date and his parents' names and my friend promised to give me the information so I could get a copy of his birth certificate, which, for some reason, he seemed unable to do.

On Friday, 19th April, Maria appeared at the gate.

"*Hola* Lindsay, I have the information for you on Pedro," she said, handing me a piece of paper.

"Oh brilliant, now I can get Pedro's birth certificate, which will make Lynne very happy as they need that for the wedding," I said, relieved.

"But she cannot marry him," replied Maria, looking a little confused. "He is married already."

"He is what?" I screamed.

"Yes, look, you can see it all here. I have written it down. He married this woman – she is called Kayleigh Annabel Peters. She is from Canada and they married on 17th July, 2012."

I was shocked, that was the day Lynne had flown here with her family, when Pedro was supposedly off training. But the massive problem was how on earth I was going to tell her? Lynne had been on her own for years – her husband had left when her adult sons were only toddlers – and it had taken her all that time, around twenty years, to trust and love again, and now I was about to break her heart.

It took me a couple of hours, and a couple of rums, to summon up the courage to type to her using Facebook messenger.

Me: Hi, how goes it.

Lynne: Fine and you?

I'm OK. *Here we go.* I have the information on Pedro's birth certificate.

Brilliant, thanks so much. When will you be able to go and collect the actual certificate? Everything is planned for the wedding. The cake is ordered, I have my dress, the tickets are booked, rings bought, I have arranged the wedding supper. All we need are his papers. Thanks so much for helping.

Oh bloody hell, I thought

> Well there is a little problem and I really don't want to have to tell you.

> Tell me what? Tell me!

(taking a deep breath and another swig of rum).

> There won't be a wedding. He is already married. Well, that is what the Civil Registry says.

There was a pause and Lynne didn't reply straight away. Then she did.

> Give me her name.

> I have the name, but I won't give it to you yet, let me research it as there may be a mistake.

> Why not? This is killing me. I need to know who she is. When did they get married?

> 17th July 2012

> OMG. I was there. He couldn't come as he said he was training. Even his family was late arriving.

> Let me check this woman out first, okay.

Okay but do it fast, and break it to me gently.
Do we know who the witnesses were?

I searched on Facebook, but I couldn't find her.

Okay I have looked, but I can't find her on Facebook. Do you want to try? And no, the Civil Registry does not have the witnesses' names.

Sure give me her name and I will look.

This is the name, Kayleigh Annabel Peters. She is Canadian and was married at 3.20pm on 17th July 2012.

Should I ask him about it?

Well, I would speak to her first, if you can find her.

Ten minutes went by.

I have found her. And yes, she is with him, and OMG they have a son. Should I ask him about her now?

I don't know Lynne. When are you coming back here as over the phone will be hard. Why don't you try and message her first, or do you want me to?

I don't know what to do, we talked about this. How I needed a man who was faithful. What should I do? I don't know what to do. OMG. What the hell should I do?

I am so sorry. I feel awful.

I will have to ask him. I was planning on coming in May to make the final wedding plans. My flight is booked.

Well, come anyway and come and see me.

Should I?

I think so. You need to talk to him and get closure.

I spoke to him earlier and told him I didn't like problems and he said there will be no more problems now, and now this.

I just don't know what to do. What should I message her?

Do you want me to message her?

Would you mind?

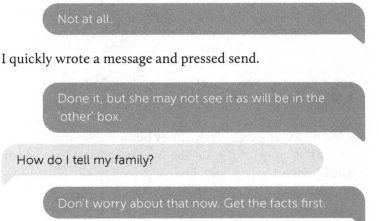

> Not at all.

I quickly wrote a message and pressed send.

> Done it, but she may not see it as will be in the 'other' box.

> How do I tell my family?

> Don't worry about that now. Get the facts first.

I sent Kayleigh a message saying I needed to talk to her and she came back to me a couple of days later.

Kayleigh: Hello! I'm guessing we need to talk about Pedro. I'm sorry I'm not replying till now. Didn't even know that I had these messages on here. I would love to hear what you have to say!

Me: Hi Kayleigh, yes, it was about Pedro, and was just to confirm that you were married to him as a friend of mine was due to marry him in August.

She was what? Yes, I am married to him. He is supposed to come here to live with myself and his four-year-old son at the end of the month. I had no idea he had a girlfriend. Is she Canadian too?"

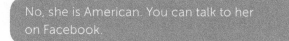

> No, she is American. You can talk to her on Facebook.

Yes, I will. Mind you, I'm not sure if I'll even pick him up from the airport now!

She didn't seem particularly upset but a week later I heard the familiar 'ping' of the Facebook message and once again it was Lynne.

Lynne: OMG

> **Me:** Now what.

He has another one, she is British. They were due to marry in February, but he said that his papers weren't ready. That is when I couldn't get hold of him for three weeks, when he said his phone was broken.

> That is definitely an OMG. How did you find out?

She liked the Chivirico page and her profile picture is her with Pedro. I have messaged her and she messaged me back. This is what she said. Her name is June.

June: This is horrible. I'm so sorry for you Lynne. You know you hear stories and family and friends warn you, but you believe in your heart that no, he is not like that. I let the little warnings slide and made excuses as he is from a different culture. You believe in him, he says all the right things, you love him and then one day you find out that he has been lying for the whole relationship. It's heartbreaking and embarrassing that I have let myself deny red flags.

Right now he is sending me messages, not many, but saying he loves me and asking if I'm okay! Really he still chooses not to say anything about the mother of his child or his child!! I confronted him with her name and he denied knowing her and then asks me if I'm okay! I will give him the opportunity to tell me the truth and see what he says. I'm also telling him I will not be sending money any more.

So it appears that Pedro decided to cover the bases and was engaged to a Brit, a Canadian and an American at the same time and probably planned to marry all three and then see which one got him a visa first. Meanwhile each of the ladies was planning their wedding, each sending him money for his passport, for a new phone, for any disaster he had. This type of Dominican man did not seem to realize that the Civil Registration and Electoral Office had a new system, and instead of marriages just being registered locally in a book in the local office, they were now kept centrally and computerized. Previously, they would marry a foreign lady who would return home and then should the relationship not work out, or should they not get a visa, then they would just marry another one in a different office.

Unfortunately, due to the new computerized system when he came to marrying the Brit, June, he discovered his little problem.

He flew to Canada to join his wife. Lynne never spoke to him again and, once he had left the country, nor did June, although she spent some time believing him when he said he would go to Canada, but only for six months then would divorce his Canadian wife and come back and marry her. His whole family was in on the scam as all of the women would spend time in his family home with his mother and sisters. Facebook messages went backwards and forwards for weeks until he went to Kayleigh in Canada, denied having any relationship with Lynne and June and Kayleigh then blocked them on Facebook.

Shortly afterwards, June came on the holiday she already had booked to see him – which was at the same time he was due to marry Lynne – and met another Dominican who she later married and took to England.

Lynne had planned to come in May to make the final arrangements for the wedding and she decided to come anyway and try and speak to Pedro face to face at the hotel where he worked on the east coast. She also arranged to come and stay with me for a few days and asked if it would be possible to have a whole roasted pig, which is a Dominican tradition. The only problem was that we didn't have a barbecue to cook it on, so I asked Danilo to build one.

"Hey, Danilo, we need to build a little barbecue so that we can cook a little pig on it for Lynne. All you need to do is get a few cement blocks, and a grill and that will do." I emphasized the word 'little' as I know how Danilo can get carried away.

"I build barbecue, no problem," he replied confidently, and disappeared into the garden to start the planning. There is nothing Danilo liked more than planning a new project. He worked out the size in his head and arranged to have the metal bits made – the grill and the spit for the pig. In the meantime, I was duly dispatched to buy cement, sand, gravel, metal bars (not sure what they were for) wood, a shark-tooth saw and nails.

I drove up to the mountain town of Monción in my little old Jeep, admiring the stunning mountain scenery on the way. Monción was around eleven kilometres away on a windy road with sheer drop-offs. The sides of the road were lined with trees, bougainvillea, and beautiful red and yellow flames trees. To the right in the distance you could see the outline of the mountains in Haiti and to the left and ahead, the towering peaks of the central mountain range of the Dominican Republic. I could not help but feel uplifted as I made the journey, dodging the potholes in the road and waving at the old men on their donkeys.

Monción had one main street and very few shops. There was one bank, a veterinary supply shop – mostly for farm animals – Western Union and Caribe Express to receive money people sent from overseas, one clothes shop and several general stores and pharmacies. Danilo had given me strict instructions on what to buy, so I strode confidently into the one and only supermarket, which was also the one and only hardware store. I walked up to the counter at the back and was faced by a long line of men in blue coats, who scrabbled to serve me.

"*Hola,*" I said smiling, and looking down at my list. "Five bags of cement please."

The oldest of the men had won the competition to serve me, and he entered something into what seemed like a big computer.

"Five bags of cement. Anything else?"

"Yes, I need twenty metres of sand and ten metres of gravel." Danilo had explained that sand and gravel are sold by the metre, which seemed most odd to me.

"We don't sell sand and gravel by the metre," the man explained.

"Oh. So what do you sell them by?" I replied, thinking that I had thought metres was a stupid measurement for sand and gravel.

"By the wheelbarrow,"

Well, that makes sense. Not. I thought.

"How many metres in a wheelbarrow, or how many wheelbarrows in a metre?" I asked

"No idea," he responded helpfully. "If you want a lot of wheelbarrows you can buy it in a different way."

"Which way might that be? Metres," I enquired hopefully.

"No. You can have a full lorry load, a half load or a quarter load."

"How many wheelbarrows in a quarter load?" I asked trying by now not to laugh.

"No idea," he answered.

"How big is the lorry then?"

"Lorry sized."

We were not making much progress so I ordered a quarter of a lorry of gravel and half of sand and just hoped the lorry was not a juggernaut. The next thing on the list was metal bars, which he explained were to strengthen the concrete. The metal bars are sold by the quintal. In India and Albania, the quintal is equivalent to a hundred kilogrammes. In France it used to be a hundred pounds, but is now a hundred kilogrammes. In Portugal a quintal is a hundred and twenty-eight pounds and in the Dominican Republic a hundred pounds.

"Can I please have a quarter of a quintal of metal bars?" That was no problem.

I also needed nails, which were sold by the pound and once all was entered into the computer, I paid and then with my bag of nails in hand I went home and waited for the delivery of the rest of the stuff. Once everything was delivered later in the day, it sat in the front garden for a few weeks, much to the delight of the cats, who had the biggest litter tray in the world with the pile of sand. Eventually Danilo started work on the barbecue, but it wasn't ready for Lynne's visit in May, she had to wait until December for her pig.

Lynne flew into Punta Cana and spent a few painful days at the hotel where Pedro worked. She didn't see him as he was supposedly on holiday, so was unable to confront him about what he had done. Later it came to light that his boss, who obviously knew about all of his women, had warned him to keep out of the way so he was there at the hotel, but stayed in the staff quarters until Lynne left to come and see me.

As we lived on the other side of the island, she caught a domestic flight to Santiago airport. It was supposed to be a nineteen-seat plane, but Dominican maths not being the best, it had a seat next to the pilot and a bench seat behind which could take three people at a squash. The luggage was thrown behind the bench seat.

As Lynne sat nervously in the plane wondering if she would make it to Santiago in one piece, Danilo, Chivirico and I made the two-hour journey to the airport. We got to the arrivals hall in plenty of time and the loudspeaker system announced that the plane had landed at 3.15pm, right on time. But an hour later, at 4.15pm, there was still no sign of her, and only one other person waiting at arrivals, so we asked a nice man who said that domestic flights came into another terminal. Back to the car and we drove at top speed to the supposed other terminal, where we were told it was only used for private planes and not domestic ones. Back in the car and back to general arrivals. Still no sign of her, so I walked up to the information desk.

"Hello, I'm waiting for someone on a domestic flight from Punta Cana and there is no sign of her."

"The plane hasn't landed yet," the uniformed woman replied, unsmilingly.

"Well, the public announcement said that it landed at 3.15pm and that was nearly two hours ago now."

"You shouldn't listen to that. It's a tape recording. We have one for each day and it makes the announcement that the plane has landed when it was supposed to land. It doesn't mean the plane has landed."

"Err... that seems a tad strange and it said 'We would like to announce the arrival of...'."

"We can't afford the wages for a live person. Let me ask the control tower. They are the only ones who know when planes have landed." And with that she spoke into her walkie-talkie and turned back to me. "Yes, it has just landed, she will be through soon."

Five minutes later Lynne walked through the doors, to be met by Chivirico who ran up to meet her, throwing his arms around her. No one could resist a Chivirico cuddle.

We had a lovely few days and in no time at all we drove her back to Santiago for the perilous flight back to Punta Cana, knowing we would meet again in August when she came with her family to the villa for the wedding which was not going to happen, but the holiday would go ahead as the flights and the villa could not be cancelled. Chivirico, Danilo and I had been invited to the wedding so we would go for the weekend.

Life in the campo continued to be interesting and even though I had lived in the country for years, every day in this environment I was learning new things. There were many visitors at the gate, and one day Danilo had gone into Monción to pay the electricity bill but we had no idea how much it was as we hadn't had a bill – nothing out of the ordinary really. We had electricity twenty-four hours a day, but where we lived before the bill was never more than RD$1,200 and was also charging the twelve-battery inverter for half of the time, so I expected it to be around the same even though we now had a proper fridge and a freezer.

Around fifteen minutes later there was a shout at the gate. It was an electricity man in the uniform of the local electricity company, Edenorte, with a white hard hat and the all important clipboard.

"I have come to investigate the complaint," he announced.

"What? What complaint? Who is complaining?" I replied, somewhat shocked.

"The office rang me so I have come to investigate. Where is your husband?"

"He went to the electricity company to pay the bill," I replied.

"Well, I am here to investigate the complaint. How much was the bill?"

"What bill? We have no bill? And who complained about what?" I asked in utter bemusement.

"Your husband complained when he saw the bill," he explained. "So the office rang me and I am here to investigate. How much was the bill?"

"I have no idea as my husband is still not home, and I haven't seen the bill."

"Well, don't worry, I can come into the house and look at what you have and tell you what the bill should be."

By this stage Hector was at the gate and frantically trying to shake his head at me without moving it.

"Sure, come on in," I said with a smile. "You don't mind dogs do you?"

"What dogs?" he asked, and on cue Belinda and Silly Boy ran into the garden, pulled themselves up to their full height and put their nasty faces on.

Faced with a Great Dane and an English Mastiff, Mr. Electricity Man went slightly pale.

"No, that's fine, just tell me what electrical items you have," he said with his pen hovering over his clipboard.

"Well," I said, watching Hector looking concerned out of the corner of my eye as he knew English women do not tell fibs.

"We have a little (ahem) fridge. A washing machine."

"American?" he interrupted. "Washer dryer?"

"No, a Dominican plastic one," I replied. "We have a computer, well a lap top, and a television." I conveniently forgot the other two televisions and the freezer. "Oh, and a microwave, and that's it."

"No fan? "

"No. It's not hot enough.'

"No stereo system"

"No," piped up Hector

And that was that. The bill was actually RD$4,000 pesos, which was very high, but we discovered there was something wrong with the inverter, which was constantly charging the batteries, so we turned it off and the bill went down to a much more manageable RD$1,200 pesos around £20.

A few days later there was another shout at the gate and this time it was a lady in a white coat riding side-saddle on the back of a motorbike.

"*Hola*," I said, as I approached the gate, wondering what on earth it was this time.

She also had a clipboard and a big basket of what looked like the old fashioned thin cardboard medical files, which we used to have in England when I was a child.

"Good morning, *buenas*. Danilo Feliz Torres?" she enquired, looking at her clipboard.

"He isn't here. I'm his wife," I answered nervously. "What's all this about."

"I am the doctor from the Polyclinic. I have come to do the examination."

"The what clinic? And what examination? Who is being examined?"

"You are."

"I am? What are you examining me for?"

"The Polyclinic is in Cepillo (which means Brush) between here and Monción. It is open Monday to Friday from 8am in the morning to noon. It is all free, including medicines and we do TB tests, blood tests and cervical smears. I am here to take your medical record."

"Oh," I said in surprise. "Do you want to come in?"

She looked at the dogs who were in the doghouse.

"Err, no I don't think so, thank you. Do you have any illnesses?"

"High blood pressure that's it," I replied, and she wrote something down on what was to be my file.

"No diabetes, heart problems?"

"No."

"That is the end of your examination. Thank you. Please call into the clinic to be weighed and have your blood pressure taken." And with that she hopped precariously onto the back of the motorcycle – whose rider had been listening intently to my answers – and off they bounced down the rutted track.

A few weeks later I was sitting at my computer when I heard the big metal entrance gate being slid back and I peered out of the window to see Hector opening it and a large white car driving in. *Who the hell is it?* I wondered, feeling apprehensive, as we still hadn't let on to anyone exactly where we were living, I just said we lived in the middle of nowhere.

Hector walked in through the front door,

"There are two people here to see you," he announced.

"Well, who the hell are they?" I hissed back at him.

"*No se*. I have no idea," he replied. "They asked if Lindsay de Feliz lived here and I said yes."

I wandered outside, somewhat nervously and the well-dressed, middle-aged woman clambered out of the car and screamed.

"It is her, Jorge, look it is her. Oh my God!"

I walked slowly up to the car feeling even more nervous, waiting to be shot and having no idea what they wanted. The couple came towards me, smiles beaming all over their faces and the man, Jorge, shook my hand warmly.

"I cannot believe we have found you!" he said. "Our daughter will be so happy. She lives in Chile and follows your blog, but cannot buy your book there and she is desperate to read it. You posted on your blog a photograph of a man on a donkey and she called us and asked us to look at it and yes, it was great uncle Bututo! So she said he must know you so we have driven here from Santiago to try and find you and ask you to sell us a copy of *What About Your Saucepans?*"

His wife chimed in. "And so we went to Bututo's house and he told us where you lived and so here we are and please, *please* can we buy a copy of your book and take a photograph with you? It will make our daughter so very happy."

I was more than happy to oblige, but so much for our idea of not letting anyone know where we lived.

Work on the barbecue continued apace. A frame was made out of wood and filled with cement with the metal bars in it and various items were put in the cement to make air holes – empty bleach bottles. The barbecue I had imagined was nothing like the one I was getting – this one was not only big enough for a suckling pig, it was big enough for a cow or an elephant. There was space underneath to store the charcoal or the wood, and even that was large enough for Hector to move into.

Before moving to the *campo* I thought I knew most of what there was to know about the country, but I was very wrong. People acted differently here, they looked different and they spoke differently. I found it hard at the beginning to understand them. Sukin lived next to Barbara and Miguel with his one legged wife Leida. She had only one leg due to diabetes and so did her sister, Esterlina, who lived up the road with Bututo her husband. We had actually bought our house and land from Esterlina's sons. Everyone was related to everyone else around here, apart from Danilo and me. They were also all-white Dominicans and those who were not white were nearly white, as most were directly descended from the Spaniards, who arrived for the first time on the north coast only about fifty miles away as the crow flies.

Sukin was large, mid-fifties and had a little tiny concrete shed on the main road in his front garden. That was our local *colmado*. He stocked cigarettes, rum, and Gatorade just for me, and sold the usual staples such as rice, beans, corn (for the chickens as everyone had chickens) flour, plantains and some tins of stuff like beans, Carnation milk, sweetcorn and sardines. Every morning I would walk round to the *colmado* through Barbara's garden and then through his garden as everyone just walked through everyone else's garden – apart from ours because of the dogs. He would always say exactly the same thing as he hoisted himself up from his rocking chair on his front terrace.

"*Ay Lindsay. Ay soy ta bravo.*" What he was actually saying was "*El sol esta bravo*" or "The sun is hot" but in this part of the country the letter 'l' was pronounced as a 'y' as was the letter 'r'. Interesting to say the least and it took me a while to learn to understand it.

In addition, there were a whole range of different activities and traditions I came across. One morning at 4am, I was in the middle of a beautiful sleep, snuggled under my two quilts as it was a tad chilly in the mountains being December by now, with just the odd rooster being confused and thinking it was dawn and crowing, and suddenly there was this appalling noise from the road and the house in front of us. Shouting and singing and music and banging of drums. Our dogs started barking like crazy.

"Danilo, Danilo, what's going on?" I asked. "What on earth is all that noise in the middle of the night? Is someone dead?"

"*Los aguinaldos,*" he grunted and went back to sleep putting the pillow over his head.

"Los whatdos?"

94

There was no way I was getting out of bed to look the word up in a dictionary so I lay there and listened to them singing in Spanish.

> "*Si no te levantas, y me abres la puerta,*
> *estaré cantando, hasta que amanezca;*
> *Allá dentro veo, un bulto tapao,*
> *no se si será un lechón asao.*"

Which means in English:

> "If you don't get up nor open the door
> I will be here singing until you wake up.
> Over there I can see, over there I can see (looking through the window)
> A bag all closed up and I am thinking
> That it has a roast pig in it."

As I lay there listening to this, over and over again, I thought, *what burglars would sing outside a house where they wanted to nick a dead pig?*

Eventually, after about thirty minutes, they moved off, but I could hear them all the way down the road singing the same song and banging on the drums.

In the morning, all was explained. It was *los aguinaldos*, which means Christmas bonus and it is a Christmas tradition, especially in the countryside. Groups of people get up well before dawn and go round the neighbourhood banging on doors, playing music and singing the very same song. You are supposed to get up, even though it is in the middle of the night, and give them ginger tea and biscuits.

Apparently they didn't come to our house as they were scared of the dogs. Oh dear, what a shame, as I would have loved to have been woken up at 4am to make ginger tea and biscuits for people who are looking for a dead pig in a sack.

I suppose it is like the British carol singing tradition, but not quite the same as angelic children singing Christmas carols in the early evening.

As Christmas approached another custom was explained. We were supposed to clean the whole house, wash it all out and mop it and then paint it before Christmas and burn all our old clothes and get new ones. We are supposed to put all our old brushes and mops and brooms out at the corner of the street and buy new ones. Again I think not – I can feel this *gringa* is going to get a reputation as being a tad bolshie!

My biggest client, Jonathan, lived in the capital, Santo Domingo, and whilst we communicated by email, Skype and phone, every few months we would meet up for the weekend to work. We had a system in that one time I would travel by bus to Santo Domingo and the next time he would come closer to me.

This particular time he decided to come to me and we would stay in Mao, which was only twenty minutes or so from me and, amazingly, had a five-star hotel. Well, it said it was five-star. It was also used for training hotel and catering students.

As he ran a hotel in Santo Domingo and was fanatical about excellent customer service I checked there were no events going on while we were there, so it would be nice and peaceful. They also guaranteed they had excellent service. Lying sods.

I should have realised things would not go smoothly as driving to the hotel I had yet another puncture. This time on the road between Los Quemados, which was around two miles from us and at the bottom of the hill, and Mao, where there is no phone signal and very little traffic. Usually when you have a puncture Dominicans will stop straight away, but not on this road as it is known for people pretending to break down and then robbing their rescuers at gunpoint. So, not a good place to have a puncture. Also, I had an elderly lady in the car who I was giving a lift to, which was just as well as – seeing that no one was stopping – she fearlessly walked into the middle of the road and held up the traffic until a man on a motorbike and a man with a truck full of bananas stopped and helped us.

The tyre was changed and off we went again and I dropped her where she wanted to go and went to wait at the bus station for Jonathan. Suddenly Danilo turned up as someone had seen me from a passing bus when I was stranded, trying to stop the elderly lady from being run over in the middle of the road. This person had called him and told him what had happened. He had left university, checked to see if I was at the hotel, and was checking the bus station before driving up the road to see if I was still stranded and rescue me. Talk about jungle drums.

I picked up Jonathan and we went to the hotel, but the area by the pool was full of students having their pictures taken for graduation.

I walked up to reception. "Excuse me, but when I booked I asked if you had any events going on this weekend and you said you didn't."

"This isn't an event," replied the snooty receptionist. "This is photography."

Every time the photographer took a picture his flash blew the hotel's electricity and all the power went off. He took a lot of pictures and the power kept going off.

Jonathan had no towels and his fridge didn't work. There was no hot water and worst of all there was no Internet. I went to reception.

"My friend has no towels, his fridge doesn't work, there's no Internet and no hot water. This is supposed to be a five-star hotel!"

The receptionist said it would be sorted, but it took till the next day for the Internet to be working and even then it kept going off. Luckily, we both had USB sticks. The water was never hot and the fridge was never fixed.

The next morning we went down for breakfast and the buffet was remarkably uninspiring, so we asked for an omelette.

"No problem, and what would you like in the omelette?" enquired the pleasant waitress.

"Mushrooms and bacon," Jonathan said.

"Same for me please," I said, with my mouth watering at the idea of real mushrooms.

"Yes, we can do that," replied the waitress, and off she went. She came back a minute or so later.

"There is a problem," she announced.

"No mushrooms?" I said aghast.

"Yes, we have mushrooms," she replied, and I breathed a sigh of relief.

"No bacon?" asked Jonathan.

"Yes, we have bacon."

It was my turn. "Oh my God, no eggs?"

"Yes, we have eggs. But the problem is that the free breakfast included in the room rate only includes the buffet."

Jonathan said, "I think my budget can stretch to two omelettes." So the waitress smiled and left.

It was relief all round until the omelettes arrived. They did have bacon and mushrooms – but they also had cheese, onions, tomatoes, potatoes. Jonathan didn't eat cheese ever, or onions, for breakfast.

"I asked for a bacon and mushroom omelette," he complained.

"Well, what an omelette is, is eggs with everything else. An omelette is not just eggs," the waitress explained.

The issue of being served with food you had not asked for continued. The chicken sandwich, which the menu said had chicken and salad, came with ham, cheese, slathered in mayonnaise and without the chicken. Having sent it back three times it eventually came out right.

We had planned to work by the pool, but it was impossible as the photographer was still there – along with hundreds of graduates.

In the end the hotel gave us a meeting room, but only for a few hours. Discussions with the manager proved useless – when Jonathan wanted to swim, but couldn't as there were so many people, she said that if you go to the beach there are a lot of people. He pointed out you didn't pay nearly US$80 a day to go to the beach. She promised the photographer would finish at 4pm. He did. She didn't mention he would start again at 6pm and go on most of the night.

The following day we went back for breakfast again. The buffet table was empty.

"Where is breakfast?" I asked the waiter. He waiter pointed to a table of ten Dominicans.

"They moved all the buffet onto their table so they don't have to keep getting up and down," he explained.

"So, what about our breakfast?" asked Jonathan.

"Just go and help yourself from their table," replied the waiter. Which is what we did.

I was grateful to get back to peace and quiet in the mountains; however, one of the cats was missing – Bubbly. He was part of a black pair of cats, Bubble and Squeak, or Bubbly and Quees as Danilo called them, but Squeak had been poisoned in the pink house along with five other cats. Bubbly was very friendly and did tend to wander off a bit so I wasn't too concerned, but as the days passed and there was no sign of him I asked Danilo and Hector to investigate. Later that day we sat down for lunch and I asked if they had any news.

"Yes," said Hector. "Bubbly is in the *Barrio de los Acotaos*."

A *barrio* is a neighbourhood and most towns have several, with names like *Barrio Lindo* (Pretty neighbourhood), *Barrio Duarte* – named after one of the founding fathers – and they can also have what are, to us, strange names such as *Barrio los Chicharrones*, which is Pork Scratchings' neighbourhood.

I am well used to odd place names, so I said, without really thinking what it meant,

"Where is *Barrio de los Acotaos*?"

"Over there," said Hector, waving his arm in the general direction of the wood.

"Well, he will be home soon," I said confidently.

"Err, I don't think so," interrupted Danilo. "No one returns from *Barrio del los Acotaos*."

"Why on earth not?" I asked. "Well, I'll just go and get him then. Now where exactly is it?"

There was silence, and then I thought about the name. *Acotao* was probably really *acostado*, which means sleeping, laying down – *policia acostado* are sleeping policemen in the road or speed bumps. Bubbly was in the sleeping neighbourhood.

"Bubbly is dead," announced Danilo, in a matter of fact way. "He was playing with some baby chicks in the next *campo* to us and the owner was not happy about it, so he shot him with a shotgun."

Rest in Peace, Bubbly, in the *Barrio de los Acotaos*. Over the next year or so most of the cats went to the *Barrio de los Acotaos*. Some disappeared, one was run over, and some were poisoned by, I assume, the neighbours. We were eventually left with only two, fifteen-year-old Zebedee who was blind and five-year-old Mariposa. One thing I was learning about the *campo* is that as well as being beautiful with what I thought were some strange habits, it could also be unforgiving when it came to any animals that were not chickens.

The *campo* continued to delight me. We had no air conditioning and no fans as it was always cool in the summer and downright cold in the winter with temperatures dropping to 50° Fahrenheit at night. I would get up early, around 6am, and watch the hummingbirds in the garden, sipping my freshly made coffee before starting work for the day.

Danilo continued to fix up the house, installing a gymnasium in the front garden, made from tree trucks and concrete – set in large plastic paint buckets for the weights, and he and Hector spent many an hour out there working out when Danilo was not at university. I was working hard, marketing the book and travelling to launches and book clubs around the country, writing articles and being interviewed by different expat websites. I was also being contacted more and more by ladies wanting help with their relationships with Dominican men. Life could not get much better and at last I felt totally at peace.

Chivirico would come most weekends and we would cook and bake together and at night he and I would take the dogs out into the back garden for their nightly walk, his little hand tightly holding mine and we would stop and stand and stare up at the stars. There were no lights at all so the stars were amazing.

"Look, Chivirico, there is my dad," I would say.

"And there is your grandma," he would reply, pointing up to the dark velvet sky. "And there is Tyson, and Fred, and Sophie," he would carry on pointing excitedly. When his great grandmother died he was desperate to run outside at night and see if he could see her.

"Look, there is one more star tonight!" he exclaimed, pointing up at the thousands of stars. "That's great grandma."

I could buy day-to-day products at Sukin's *colmado*, and around a mile away in the centre of the village there was a little supermarket and a vegetable shop. In addition, there was an old-fashioned department store selling household goods, clothes, fabric and toys. It reminded me of Grace Brothers which used to be on British television back in the Seventies. There was an upstairs, with a steep wooden staircase and any customer who went upstairs was escorted by a very large elderly gentleman. He grew to hate me as I would always wander upstairs for a look around, and I could hear him puffing and panting his way behind me on the stairs. He was even more annoyed if I didn't buy anything. There was also a pork butcher who killed a pig every Saturday, then rang a bell when it was ready – which we could hear where we lived. He would stay open until he had sold all of his pig. Apart from pork, the only other meat available was chicken and there was no fish. Many basic ingredients were not available, so I had to become especially inventive. I made my own pizzas from scratch, my own bread, and cooked a lot of Thai food using what was available such as ginger, lemon grass, limes, garlic and chillies. Whilst it was time consuming, the end result was lovely tasting food.

I had never felt so safe in this country, in fact never felt so safe anywhere. We had no bars on the windows, no locks on the doors, and even left the front door open at night so the dogs could go outside at will. There was no crime, no violence, just a group of people helping each other out with food and produce, or whatever you needed. If I had visitors coming the local ladies would descend on my house to clean it. If you were walking up the street, someone would always give you a ride. So far the only downside I could see was that chickens and roosters were the most important animals and any cat or dog that disposed of them was swiftly dealt with by poison.

CHAPTER FIVE

CHRISTMAS IN THE CAMPO

---

*"Whatever your labors and aspirations, in the noisy
confusion of life keep peace with your soul."*
Desiderata, Max Ehrmann 1927

LYING IN BED AT NIGHT WE OFTEN HEARD NOISES ON THE ROOF
and had no idea what they were. Chivirico, who was with us
for the weekend, came into our bedroom early one morning in
his pyjamas.

"De Fe, there is something going on. There is a noise on the
roof every night. What is it? Is it a witch?"

"No, silly, it isn't a witch, there aren't any witches here," I said
sleepily, pulling my head up from under the covers.

"Well, it's something," he replied. "I am off to Barbara's to vestigate. She will know what it is." And with that he skipped down the stairs and I heard the big metal front door clang behind him.

He came back shortly after by which time I was making bread in the kitchen.

"It's a see-gwa-pah," he announced as he ran in through the door.

"What's that?" I asked, dusting the flour off my hands.

"It's a woman in the woods with backwards feet."

"Right, of course it is," I smiled, knowing this was about to be another Dominican myth. Once the bread was proving, Chivirico dragged me around to Barbara's so she could explain. She was busy at her *fogon* cooking lunch, so I perched on a nearby log while Chivirico listened intently.

"A *ciguapa* is the spirit of Taíno Indian women who used to live here before Columbus came," she explained. "They are very beautiful and look like a woman with brown or dark blue skin. They don't wear clothes, but their hair is straight and very long so it covers their bodies. They only live in the mountains, not down there in the towns," she pointed down the road then carried on. "*Ciguapas* only come out at night, but if you try to follow them it is hard as their feet face backwards so you do not know which way they have gone."

"I would love to see one," I said, fascinated.

"You never will," said Barbara all knowingly. "Only men see her, not women and not children as it is only the men she wants. If the man sees her and looks her in the eye, she is so beautiful the man will fall under her spell and he will follow her into the wood. She will have sex with him and then she kills him."

"Goodness, I had better keep an eye on Danilo then. We don't want him running off after a woman with no clothes and backwards feet for a bit of nookie, followed by certain death."

"Come on Chiv, time to cook the lunch."

By now Chivirico had eyes like saucers and went running back to the house to wake Danilo up and tell him all about the *ciguapa* who lived in the wood.

That weekend, Danilo, Chivirico and I set off for Jarabacoa for Lynne's non-wedding. I adored going on trips with Chivirico. He spoke nonstop, made friends with everyone wherever we went and his excitement was infectious.

"Are we there yet?" he asked, every two minutes. "Tell me about Jarabacoa again," he demanded.

"Well, it's in the mountains, like we are. It's known as the Switzerland of the Dominican Republic. Switzerland is a country in Europe full of mountains. We will stay in a villa, there is a swimming pool, so you can learn to swim and we will go to a restaurant which goes round and round in circles."

Chiv was bouncing up and down in the back seat of the car with excitement.

We had a fabulous time with Lynne, her sons, mum and other family and friends. We ate like kings and queens, Chivirico learned to swim and make pancakes and cup cakes and we came away laden with goodies and clothes. We also went to the restaurant with a revolving floor, which was called *Aroma de la Montaña* and where the wedding breakfast was supposed to have been – but there was no groom. And the lady who owned it had read my book!

While we were there I had time to talk to Lynne.

"How are you doing? This must be so hard as it was supposed to be your wedding," I said.

"Yes, not easy, but I'm okay. I'm so pleased you and Danilo and Chivvy are here, "she replied. "I still love this country, despite all that's happened. What are you doing for Christmas?"

"Well, we are broke as usual," I replied. "The tree never made it from Juan Dolio. I'll try and do something, but without a tree."

"I'll make sure you and Chivvy have a great Christmas, as you've helped make me have a great non-wedding," Lynne said determinedly.

As Christmas approached there was the smell of ginger in the air every evening as the eight houses in the *campo* took turns to make ginger tea on their *fogons*. And of course the *campo* Christmas tree had to be erected. I was asked if I could buy some Christmas tree lights, which I did. The tea was being made at Barbara's house and we all trooped onto the road in front of her house to put the tree on the verge at the edge of the road. All of the houses were on the left of the little main road apart from Angela's, which was opposite Barbara's. Angela lived there with her husband, Leopoldo, and their son, Christian, who was Danilo's friend. Angela was even shorter than me, although a tad more rotund, and never stopped laughing. I called her the *bruja*, or witch, as she was always cackling with laughter.

Firstly, the men hammered a big metal stake into the ground at the side of the road and then they and the ladies went around sticking bits of the tree into the stake until it looked more or less like a Christmas tree. Wires were put in place to secure it and stop it falling over and it was decorated. Finally, the lights were put on, the plugs on the lights were snipped off and the wires were fixed with taypee to an extension lead. And they worked.

Every night, leading up to Christmas, you would hear someone yell, "*Jengibre listo!*" which means 'ginger's ready' and we would all put on our coats and woolly hats – it was downright chilly – and trek out to the Christmas tree. Someone would put music on their phone and we would dance *bachata* and *merengue* under the stars on a cool December night, watching the lights twinkling on the tree and the cars beeping at us as they sped past on the road –although some would stop and come and join in with the festivities.

It was 2013, but the Christmas tree would never be put up again, nor would the ginger tea be made.

As Lynne had promised, she plotted and planned and turned up yet again. This time it was ten days before Christmas and she came laden with goodies – solar lights for the garden, garden tools, barbecue tools, things for the dogs, food, clothes and everything needed for a proper American Christmas. She had hardly walked in the door when she went off in search of a tree, decorations and a fairy, but that wasn't enough. She had bought stockings for all of us, and presents from her, her mum and members of Chivirico's Facebook page, who she had coordinated with and who had sent several gifts for her to bring.

Once the tree was sorted it was off to buy groceries for Chiv's grandparents and then we set off for the forty-five minute drive to the *barrio* in Esperanza to deliver them to him, along with US$150 collected by his Facebook fans. Grandmother was delighted to see us and we hauled the big boxes of goodies through the tiny living room onto the wooden table in the kitchen. Chivirico was in charge of taking things out of the cardboard boxes.

"We have rice," he yelled. "Beans, porridge, Maggi stock cubes..." and everything was taken out and handed over to Grandmother, who looked at it, then put it down on the table as she stood there with a large grin on her face. Once again they would have a proper Christmas Eve supper. We drank the obligatory cup of strong sweet coffee and then Chivirico jumped excitedly into my Jeep and came back with us to help prepare for the pig roast, which we had promised and as the barbecue was ready all we needed was the pig.

We decided a twenty-five pound pig would be fine, so Danilo was duly dispatched to find the pig. Somewhere along the line he invited people from his university, as well as some of the neighbours – Margarita, her brother Berto, dad Feluche, and her two teenage girls who had the house in front of ours, which faced the main road. The little meal for just us grew in the usual Danilo fashion. And somewhere along the line the twenty-five pounds was lost in translation and he came back and announced he had bought the pig. It was eighty pounds and would be delivered the next day, alive.

I was unimpressed and even more unimpressed when told I was to cook the inedible bits for the dogs.

"No way, José"

"My name is Danilo, *no es José*," he said, grinning.

"I can think of a lot more names to call you, plonker. I do not kill pigs. I do not cook pig bits for dogs. Now sort it. I want a little pig, I want a dead pig, I want a cleaned pig and I want a shaved pig, as I am not shaving it either."

"*Que es un plonker?*"

"Shut up."

The following night a horn honked at the gate

"*Quien?*"

"It's the pig," a man's voice shouted.

I walked to the gate full of dread with Chivirico trotting behind me with a knife, which he said he would use to kill the pig, but said pig was dead, on the back of a motorbike, and clean without bits and shaved – thank goodness.

That night the pig was seasoned ready for the next day and wrapped in leaves from a banana tree. We got up early and were faced with technical hitch number one. You are supposed to light the charcoal first, wait for the flames to die down and for it to be glowing red, then put the pig on. But the roasting pole went through two holes at the side of the barbecue with no way of lowering the pole from the top, so you had to put the pole in one hole and slide the pig onto it which would mean standing on top of the charcoal and more than the pig would be barbecued.

Given Danilo didn't fancy his bits being crispy, the pig had to go on first, then the fire lit. The pig then charred a bit – well, a lot – but in the end all was well, although the Dominicans howled at me with laughter sticking my meat thermometer in it to check it was cooked.

So, all in all it was a great week. Lynne ate Indian curry for the first time, made pizzas from scratch, no packets, no tins, no jars, ate lentils for the first time, ate peas and pumpkin from our garden, used a Dominican washing machine for the first time, and, I think, realised how easy and time saving appliances and shopping are in the first world as opposed to the third world.

Although we had not really planted that many vegetables, the garden when we arrived was full of pea trees – pigeon peas. When the peas were ready, as is the custom here, we invited the neighbours over to help pick them as they are a vital part of the Christmas Eve meal. *Moro con guandules* is rice with peas. They picked several and taught me how to tell when they are ready – which is when the pods are fat and they are just starting to turn yellow. You also have to pick the ones that have gone brown as, although the peas are dried inside you can still use them, you just have to soak them over night. I used them like I use lentils to make *dhal*.

But although we picked a lot, the trees were still full and it was obvious the pea picking would continue for a few weeks more. However, help came from an unexpected source. I looked out of the window and there at the far end of the garden was a cow, with one of those white birds with her.

Danilo and I went to investigate and shooed her off. You just shout at cows and they leave, apparently, which is just as well as these were the biggest cows I have ever seen and I am not a cow person. The following morning the dogs were barking about two hundred metres away from the house and I looked out of the window. Obviously the cow had taken a shine to me – or more likely the peas – and had returned, inviting all her friends and relations around to join her for breakfast. There were now eight cows and three calves in the garden and they were all eating my peas.

There was no way we could shoo away so many and make sure they all went in the same direction, so we called in the assistance of the cow dogs, Meg and Belinda, and together we managed to get rid of them, with me bringing up the rear as, to be honest, I really did not want to get that close to a cow who wasn't behind a fence.

Danilo found the owner and warned him that the next time we would keep and sell the cows, as not only did they eat peas, they also ate mango and avocado trees so they were not really welcome visitors. Made me laugh though, less peas to pick and I now knew how to round up cows – in theory.

In our drive for self-sufficiency we decided to keep chickens for eggs. I had never eaten a fresh egg before I came to the *campo*, but around three miles away, on the way to Monción, if you turned left down a dirt track you would arrive at a nunnery. It was truly beautiful, standing high on the hill, a white building with a church attached, on top of which was a belfry with a shiny brass bell inside. All around were mountains and it was exactly like a scene out of *The Sound of Music*. The nuns sold trays of eggs and fresh yoghurt and cheese, and I would go there every couple of weeks. You never saw the nuns, as they were from an order that were not allowed to be seen by mere mortals, instead you pressed a button on the wall, and a few minutes later, a voice spoke soothingly.

"Hello my child, how can I help you?"

"A tray of eggs please," I would say into the speaker on the wall, and a minute or so later a panel slid back to reveal the eggs, I took them out, put the money where the eggs had been and the panel would slide back.

"Keep the change," I would shout as I walked out.

"Thank you my child, *vaya con Dios*," the voice would echo behind me.

So, the idea of freshly laid eggs for boiled eggs and soldiers was very tempting. However, the neighbourhood chickens were left free to wander around so goodness knows how anyone could find the eggs and given that the dogs like chasing chickens I thought a chicken house would be the best solution. I found a picture of one online and showed it to Danilo.

"Danilo. I want a chicken for fresh eggs. One chicken. One little fat brown cute chicken. Or maybe two, but not more. Are you listening to me? One is one. The chickens need to have a house. I know you have never seen chickens in a house, but this is a chicken house. This is where they walk around, this is where they have their food and this is where they will lay their eggs and I can just open a little door here, and take out the eggs without having to touch the chickens, as to be honest I am not a major fan of chickens, but I love fresh eggs."

He studied the picture and announced,

"I make that house. No problem. I make house for chickens like that house."

Like an idiot I believed him and over the next week little things started to disappear from the house. Like the top of the wardrobe with three little cupboards, like towels, the odd drawer, a chopping board, but bit by bit the chicken house was made.

In the end it bore zero resemblance to the picture, but looked like it might work and I just had to open my wardrobe top cupboard on the side of it, look on top of my best towel, and there would be the eggs – if all went to plan.

The hens finally arrived with all their vaccinations done. I had no idea they had to be vaccinated against chicken flu and small pox. There were ten of them, not two. They were apparently Japanese chickens. Scraggy, no feathers around their necks and the ugliest chickens I had ever seen. It appeared we would have to wait a few months before they started laying eggs, and there were two males and eight females. Roosters were not on my list as the last thing I wanted was more crowing.

"These roosters don't crow," Danilo assured me. He lied.

Here in the *campo* everyone got up with the sunrise and was tucked up in bed by nine at night. It was beautiful and quiet – usually. As well as those of us who lived here permanently, there were two houses owned by rich Dominicans from nearby towns and they came for the occasional weekend to get away to the peace and cool of the mountains.

One night, one of these weekend visitors was in residence and it sounded like he had brought hundreds of people with him. The music was turned up so loud it was unbearable and when it got to one o'clock in the morning I gave up trying to sleep.

"Danilo, go and tell him to turn the music down. Sukin is sick in hospital with a sugar attack (he also had diabetes) and his wife Leida is on her own in the house and I know she hates noise at night."

"What you want me do?" Danilo asked.

"You have lots of things you can do. Option one, tell them it is a lack of respect for the community and please to turn the noise down."

"No can do that as man is rich and a lawyer. That is English way, it no work here."

"Okay then, option two, call the police."

"That no work as here no is police and man is rich and a lawyer."

"Okay, well cut off their electricity. Esnip the wire."

"No can do, that is no legal," he retorted. "An' you no say option four."

"What is option four?" I asked.

"Throw stones," he replied, and trotted out through the back garden in his dressing gown, torch in hand.

Five minutes later the music stopped. When he returned I asked what he had said to them.

Nothing apparently. The Dominican way to ask people to turn the music down is to throw rocks into the garden or at the house. You do it from behind a bush so they can't see it is you. Well, it worked and I was very grateful.

The chicken house began to fill up, as each time Danilo went out he came back with more birds. Three guinea fowl arrived, then two ducks, and a mature hen and mature cockerel so I could have eggs straight away. He would smuggle them into the hen house so I would not notice. As if I couldn't tell the difference between a chicken and a duck.

The new hen laid an egg – hooray, but I couldn't eat it as you have to leave an egg there or she won't lay any more apparently. The next day there were two eggs.

"Right Danilo, now can I eat that egg?"

"No, as I think best we have baby chickens first," he replied.

I was very unimpressed as the plan had been to have fresh eggs not more bloody chickens, so I stole the egg when he was out and had a fabulous poached egg on toast.

With all these birds the hen house needed to be bigger, so he had to build a new larger chicken house, which took up a massive space in the garden, with chicken wire around and in order to make the roof (as chickens fly, which I never knew) he said he had a plan. He told me the roof was under control, but I persisted wanting to understand exactly what form it would take, so I could work out which of our possessions or furniture would be turned into a hen house roof.

"It will be a *lona*" he explained.

"A tarpaulin? We can't afford that and we don't have one," I retorted.

"I make one," he smiled. "On the road up to here are many pieces of *lona* for singers."

"You mean those big signs written on fabric and nailed to posts announcing concerts?" I asked, confused.

"*Si*. I take those down in the night after they have sunged and you drive car in case someone comes so we get out quickly," he said confidently.

And that is what we did, with me as the getaway driver, and all the signs were stuck together with taypee and the ducks and some of the chickens moved into their new house. The ducks needed a pond so we buried the wheelbarrow in the ground and filled it with water, but the young chickens kept committing suicide by jumping in the water and drowning, so the ducks were dispatched with Chivirico to his grandparents' house and the wheelbarrow went back to its life as a wheelbarrow.

When Lynne was with us before Christmas she had already mentioned how she would love to visit Barahona, Danilo's birthplace, but did not want to go alone. I explained that we really did not have the money to go there as even the petrol would be US$200 at least. When she sorted the Christmas tree, and put all of the presents around it, there was an envelope addressed to Danilo and I.

"Open it now, Lindsay. I want you and Danilo to open it now," she said, the day before she left. I called Danilo, and we opened the envelope together.

"Oh my God," I exclaimed as I saw what was inside, my hand over my mouth in shock.

"What is it? What hatping?" asked Danilo.

"It is two nights at Casa Bonita hotel in Barahona. The most exclusive, beautiful, luxurious and upmarket hotel there. One where we could never afford to go, and now we are going to stay there," I said, choking back tears of emotion.

Lynne and another friend, Grace, had paid for it, and all was sorted. We would be travelling with Chivirico and Lynne to Barahona along with Grace and her Dominican husband, Nany. I had met Grace, or Gray as Danilo called her, via the DR1 website. She was an American of Italian descent from Brooklyn, with a very strong Brooklyn accent – cawfee, not coffee. Gray was in her mid-sixties with long light brown hair usually scraped back off her head and had been married to Dominican, Nany, a cuddly bear of a man, for around forty years. They lived in New Jersey most of the time, but came for the winter to a *finca* they had in San Cristobal on the south coast, to the west of Santo Domingo. Grace was a perfect name for her. She was the most generous and kind person I knew, always bringing us things from the US each time she came, and not just little things, she practically kitted out our whole kitchen with a pasta machine, cutlery, bowls, plates, saucepans, as well as clothes for both of us. Nany, although he had lived in the US for years, was really like an older version of Danilo and his Dominican side came out more every time he came back to his homeland. Grace felt the same way about Nany as I did about Danilo – a combination of deep love and adoration, coupled with lots of laughter and total frustration.

The long awaited trip to Barahona arrived and Lynne flew in from the US to Santo Domingo and took a taxi to Grace and Nany's house while we picked up Chivirico, who was beginning to see more of the country than any other Dominican six-year-old and off we set on a longish (five hour) drive to San Cristobal. We spent the night there and the next morning set off in a two-car convoy to Barahona. I never tire of the drive along the south coast of the island. Most of the way the sparkling blue Caribbean Sea is on the left, and the road goes up and down like a roller coaster so the views are stupendous. On the right the scenery would change dramatically from banana plantations, to desert dotted with cacti, then sugar cane fields for miles and miles. All along the road people are selling things – massive bunches of bananas, oranges, mangos, Dominican sweets. There are little wooden shacks selling food with steaming *calderos*, iron cooking pots full of soup, or chicken and rice.

When we arrived at the hotel it was everything I had dreamed it would be. Beautiful rooms, the comfiest beds I had ever been in, with the softest sheets I had ever slept in, an infinity pool high on the hill and the ocean glistening down below. I had a room with Danilo and Lynne was with Chivirico. We swam, showered, changed and dressed for dinner and when I came out of the shower, I took a double take at Danilo.

"Danilo, we are going for dinner," I said.

"*Si*, I know. Is good as I have many hungry," he replied.

"But why are you not dressed?" I asked.

"I am dressed," he said, a little surprised.

"Yes, numpty, but you are dressed in pyjamas, the new plaid brushed-cotton pyjamas Grace bought for you," I replied, trying not to laugh. "You cannot go to dinner in a five-star hotel in pyjamas."

"I like pyjama. I eat in pyjama," he replied defiantly.

This was the first, and last, time I had been to dinner at a five-star hotel and restaurant with a man in pyjamas.

We arrived in the dining hall and looked at the menu. I read it to Chivirico while the waiter waited patiently for our order.

"There is no espaghetti," announced Chiv. "For supper my grandma always cooks spaghetti."

"Well, maybe the chef can make spaghetti for you," I said, looking hopefully at the waiter.

"Maybe Chef doesn't know how to cook spaghetti," Chivirico replied. "And I can't show him as I don't have my apron and chef hat with me."

"Perhaps you would like to come to the kitchen to discuss your requirements with the chef," suggested the waiter, kindly. And with that Chivirico got up and marched into the kitchen, returning some fifteen minutes later to announce he had taught the chef to make spaghetti, and he had decided to have prawns with it. They had lent him a chef's hat while he was cooking.

The next morning we decided to go and visit the land we had on the top of the mountain overlooking Barahona. I was really keen to go there as we had not been back for ages and Lynne really wanted to see it, too. The road used to be pretty rough and you needed a four-wheel drive vehicle, but we had been told it had been improved. They lied. Danilo was driving and says he is a brilliant driver – a *choferaso* – going forwards. He can't drive backwards. So when we got stuck going forwards, he drove backwards into the side of the mountain, with the back wheel high up on a rock, the other back wheel in a hole and one of the front wheels up in the air. The car would not budge. And it was in danger of rolling over onto its side. We all piled out of the car.

"We wait for help," said Danilo.

"We have no bloody choice, *choferaso*," I muttered.

Luckily, help arrived in the shape of a thin man on a motorcycle. Then another little man on his motorbike. This road is in the middle of nowhere so we were lucky anyone came past.

More little stick men arrived and all told us the front wheel was in the air, as if I could not see that, and all had their different plans for getting us out. None of which worked. The only solution was for them to listen to me.

"It's a waste of time pressing on the accelerator as the back wheel keeps spinning. Put the car in neutral and push it." I was ignored, until there were around fifteen little thin men all pushing in vain and two hours had passed. Then, at last, they listened to me and the car was free.

We decided not to try and make it up the hill and called it a day and headed off to the *Malecon* in Barahona. They had built a new *Malecon* – promenade in English – with a kids' playground, exercise equipment, skateboard ring, basketball court, and an old sugar train engine. While at the *Malecon* we met a friend of Danilo's who I had met before and called Sniff, as he was constantly sniffing. Danilo called him Eneef. And Lynne, after all her previous traumas, thought he was cute.

All of the time we were there in Barahona, I was a little concerned as for the previous few years Danilo was not on the phone much, but suddenly he seemed to constantly have phone calls – about politics. I was right to be concerned.

The next day we set off back on the coast road for *Bahia de las Aguilas* – Eagle Bay – supposedly the most beautiful and unspoiled beach in the Caribbean and close to Pedernales on the border with Haiti. The road was windy and dropped off on the left hand side to the clearest ocean you have ever seen. The view of the ocean was simply stunning and as you went round each corner it was more and more amazing. I was driving and Lynne was sitting next to me. Chivirico sat in the back with Danilo, who was constantly on the phone talking politics. We stopped in Enriquillo to buy a picnic lunch and continued on, the further we drove the less traffic there was. At last we turned off on a dirt track for a few miles and arrived in what looked like a little settlement. We parked the car and Danilo negotiated with a boatman to take us on his wooden fishing boat the last part of the journey to the beach. Chivirico was shaking with excitement as he was strapped into his life jacket, as he had never been on a boat before and he ran to sit at the front, held tightly by Danilo.

It is impossible to describe *Bahia de las Aguilas*. An enormous bay with the finest, whitest sand you have ever seen, with a few sea grape trees dotted around and not a soul in sight. I had never seen such clear water in my whole life, you could see the fish swimming feet below you. Not a hotel, restaurant nor café in sight. Nature at its finest. The boatman came ashore with us and joined in our picnic lunch before having his afternoon snooze. It was hard to leave such a beautiful place, but time to return to Barahona and then our mountain home.

It was not peaceful when we returned to the *campo* as our neighbours, Berto and Feluche, along with their brother who lived up the road, decided to take cock fighting more seriously and took possession of fifteen fighting cocks. They belonged to another brother of Berto who lived in the city of Santiago and his neighbours insisted he move them due to the noise. So he brought them to Berto, who lived in front of us, and due to the noise they make they housed them as far away from their house as they could – which meant they were right next to our house. They crowed all day long and drove the dogs to distraction.

"Berto, please move these cocks," I pleaded. "I can't handle the noise, no one can hear me if I call them on Skype and it is driving the dogs mad."

Berto in his usual fashion didn't answer the question. "*Todo bien?* Is everything okay?"

"No, it's not bloody okay, move these effing *maldito* cockerels," I screamed.

"They will be quiet soon," he promised. He lied.

This was also the beginning of the rainy season, which meant it rained every afternoon and whilst it was nice for the garden it was not nice for the house. The house was obviously not built for rain and water came in through every available crevice and under every door. Every afternoon, with Danilo at university, I was wandering around with my mop and bucket getting rid of the water. It seeped in under the patio doors at the back, under the front door and under the door to the doghouse. When the balcony filled with water upstairs it poured down the stairs like a waterfall and with heavy Caribbean rain falling for hours at a time, it didn't take long for the ground floor to be under six inches of water.

The only good thing about the rain is that it shut the bloody cockerels up. By now the whole neighbourhood was complaining about the noise, which went on almost twenty-four hours a day. The brother who brought the roosters here was going to be spoken to, but I did not think anything would happen, and it didn't.

Number two stepson, Alberto, got 'married' i.e. living with, which is Dominican married, to Chivirico's aunt Ana as she was pregnant and gave birth to a baby girl, Adibel, which made me a step-grandmother. She was born by Caesarean section, which is how most children are born in the Dominican Republic, weighing 7lbs 7 ounces. Not because a C-section was needed, but because the doctors want to make more money, which was exactly what happened in this case. The doctor told Ana she would not be strong enough to push the baby out and he needed to get home for his supper, so he carried out a C-section and charged RD$40,000 which is nearly US$1,000. They had insurance which covered 80% of the cost, but then had to find RD$8,000, which is more than Alberto's monthly wage and way beyond the reach of the majority of Dominicans. Family and friends usually have to come to the rescue as mother and baby were held hostage by the clinic until the bill was paid. In this case it was my mother who came to the rescue and we were all extremely grateful.

Ana stayed with her mother, Chiv's grandmother, until she was 'out of risk' or 'fuera de riesgo'. This took forty-one days, but I am not sure what she was at risk of. She had cotton wool in her ears and socks on her feet to stop cold air getting into her body and could not eat eggs or pork. She was not supposed to bathe during her 'risk time' but she did.

While I loved the *campo* at first, things were starting to go wrong, and minor frustrations, which used to make me laugh, were becoming major annoyances and what appeared to be paradise was becoming more and more difficult. The rain was an issue and storms were even worse. We had a massive storm and I was on my own most of the evening as Danilo was at university and we had fired Hector, who was doing less and less around the house and disappearing home to Bani, in the south, more and more.

When this particular storm started I ran around the house unplugging everything, as you do before a storm, and then it started. Torrential rain and massive claps of thunder with lightning all over the place. The whole garden would light up and the dogs hid under the sofa, shaking. I was concentrating on bananas to try and work out if the storm was getting closer or moving away.

"One banana, two banana," I chanted, jumping out of my skin as another massive crack of thunder made the whole house shake.

The electricity went off – it's usually turned off in a storm in case trees bring a line down and someone gets fried. One bang shook the whole house even more than before and all the windows rattled, so I wondered if we had been hit. In between mopping the water – which was coming in through every window and now up to my ankles – I was desperately trying to get an article finished for a deadline using a USB stick, rather than the Internet itself, which came in via an aerial on the roof and needed electricity and the lap top battery. I made it just as the battery died.

The electricity didn't come back on until it was dark and I only knew it was back as the shout rang out around the campo,

"*Llego la luz!*" "The electricity is back!" It had arrived everywhere else, but for some reason not in my house. A neighbour, Leopoldo, Angela's husband, came to help me investigate and he discovered the main switch was set to 'off' which I thought was odd. The switch was in the basement where a couple of hens, a cockerel and twenty-four chicks were currently living, so I thought maybe the hens had pecked it to 'off'. He switched it back to 'on' and hey presto there was light.

Until I went upstairs, which was in pitch darkness and I couldn't find the light switch. *This is most odd,* I mumbled to myself, *I know the light switch was there. Where the hell has it gone?* I sloshed back down the stairs again and went upstairs with a torch. Further investigation revealed that I couldn't find the switch as it wasn't there anymore. It had been blown off the wall, as had all the light switches and all the plug sockets. Where there were switches and sockets were now gaping holes. The Internet was fried and there had been a fire in the spare bedroom where the transformer for the modem had been. The wall was scorched brown and black and what had been the modem was now a glob of molten plastic. I had been blissfully unaware of all this activity upstairs. But there was more to come. The water pump didn't work and nor did the hot water switch, nor the Internet.

To cut a very long story short, our Internet came via a guy in Monción using a thirty-foot aerial on the roof, as there was no phone signal and no Internet line where we lived. That had been hit by lightning as, apparently, although we had asked the electrician when we moved in to put an earth in, he hadn't, and in addition there was a live wire in the garden. The electrician who came to fix it said the lightning was attracted by the live wire, hit the aerial and took out everything electrical upstairs. Luckily, as I had unplugged everything, we just needed to fix the electrics and buy a new modem, a new Internet receiver at the top of the aerial, plugs, sockets and light bulbs. The Internet was then fixed, but took a while as the Internet man, Wally, had had his phone cut off.

"Wally, you need to have your phone working, so I can contact you," I reprimanded him.

"No need. Add me to Eskippy," he replied.

"Eskippy? Eskippy is a kangaroo," I said, confused.

I had no idea what he was wittering on about until he wrote it down for me – Skype.

"That is not Eskippy, that says Skype," I explained.

"It say Eskippy. There is an 'e' at the end," Wally retorted. "And kangaroo is not Eskippy. No kangaroos here in *Republica Dominicana.*"

I gave up. Eskippy it was and Eskippy it stayed.

Danilo had been on the phone more and more discussing politics and he sat me down at the dining room table.

"I want to run for mayor again," he announced.

"Over my dead body. I am not going through that again. No. No way, never," I firmly said.

"This time will be different," he implored me. "Everyone wants me as mayor. I promise this time will work. And will help with your new book as can write about me being mayor. So it will have happy end not sad end."

"Let me think about it," I replied, having really no idea what to do. What was I to do? Deny him his dream, or say fair enough, whatever the consequences? We were fine at the moment, we didn't have much money, but we managed and his studying to be a lawyer was going well, with only around a year to go. I loved the fact he was so optimistic, but I have always wanted his unwavering optimism to be tempered with a little realism.

I know people brought up in poverty often dream impossible dreams, such as becoming a world-class baseball player or winning the lottery. My dreams when younger were achievable – a better job, a bigger house, a nicer car.

Danilo dreamed of one day having a machete like his father, but never in his wildest dreams could he imagine travelling abroad or studying at university, let alone being mayor. Unfortunately, dreaming is not sufficient to win elections and although the party confirmed they would give him all the financial support he needed after the primaries, assuming he was then elected candidate, he needed to fund the campaign up until then. So I would have to raise money just like I did before, and I really did not want to do that.

"Okay then. But I can't find any money so you have to do it yourself," I stated, knowing I would be alone a lot. No Hector, no help, but I was sure I could cope. I was wrong.

CHAPTER SIX

DR SISTERHOOD

---

*"Keep interested in your own career, however humble;
it is a real possession in the changing fortunes of time."*
Desiderata, Max Ehrmann 1927

HAVING MADE THE DECISION TO RUN FOR MAYOR, DANILO WAS
away usually for a long weekend every fortnight and, at the
same time, I lost my main job, working for Jonathan, so our
guaranteed monthly income went down to around US$150
a month, which was a tad scary. The pension had all gone
by now. That US$150 would just pay the main utility bills of
electricity, Internet, phone and television with nothing over
for food or anything else. I managed to find work writing blogs

for American attorneys, but it was tedious work which paid a pittance of US$0.01 a word, not accounting for all the research I had to do before writing the blogs. At least it was something. However, I was still helping ladies who were having issues with their Dominican husbands and boyfriends and I decided to set up a business around this.

I launched the DR Sisterhood website which enabled ladies to talk to me, Lynne, and another lady I had been helping, Jessica, along with a lady who designed the website. We were the Sisters and charged a monthly fee for constant access to chat with us, usually me, plus I would do translation of text messages and any other type of translation. In addition, we offered help with divorces, sorting any legal issues or any information about the DR. It didn't take long before the website was busy.

Jessica was a Canadian mother of three, divorced, and had a Dominican boyfriend, José. It was obvious to me from the beginning he was a sanky panky in that he was always asking for money from her, and if she refused he would become verbally aggressive and be out of contact for a while. This was a typical sanky reaction – the use of communication as a tool to control women. By the time they re-established communication, the women were usually so grateful to hear from them that they would give them the money, but it led to very destructive relationships where the women spent more time being unhappy than happy. Jessica could not understand why he had not invited her to meet his family, especially as they were discussing marriage, so she asked me to check him out. It took only twenty-four hours to discover he had a two-year-old son, although when she confronted him he swore it was his brother's and he had registered the child as his as, for some reason, the brother could not. Six months later he owned up to the child, but it took Jessica another eighteen months before she eventually cut all ties with him, by which time she had discovered he had at least another three foreign girlfriends.

Most of the women who spoke to me had low self esteem – some were overweight, most in their forties to sixties with much younger Dominican men, almost all had been divorced, some in abusive relationships. But they all had one thing in common – they were addicted to the daily texting and messaging and without it, even for twenty-four hours, they began to fall apart. If they analysed their relationship they spent more time being unhappy, desperate and on edge than they did feeling happy and cared for. They ignored red flags about the type of man they were with and time and time again I discovered these men were cheating on them, or just wanted their money. Most of the time the women ignored me and would confront their man with the information and he always had some plausible explanation.

Some of those who took their Dominican man to Canada or the US usually, although sometimes Europe, would be so scared of losing him they would place spyware on the phone and I would be sent reams of messages to translate into English. Or they would record all their phone conversations and send me tape after tape.

Some of the stories were heartbreaking, such as the man who contacted me after his wife had come to the Dominican Republic on holiday with a group of women and returned home to announce she was leaving him and their three teenage children for a barman at the hotel where she had stayed. He was supposedly single, no children, but on checking we discovered he had six kids by six different women, was married to an American and had been arrested for domestic abuse, drug dealing and possession of an illegal gun. I told the husband, he told his wife and she said we had made it up.

The sanky pankys did the same thing they always did. They had several foreign women on the go and were asking them all for money. I have never known so many disasters afflict such a group. They were constantly having supposed motorcycle accidents, or being in hospital or going to jail, and the women were always sending them money to bail them out. The scams were becoming cleverer as they would often send photos of themselves with a cast on their arm, or a drip in place – all of which were fake photos. The nasty ones would become even more manipulative and aggressive and most, although not all, of the women would submit to this.

When it came to moving, after they had married and spent a year or so waiting for the visa process to be over, they would leave for the promised land whether it be Canada or the US or Europe. Sadly, few of the relationships worked out, sometimes due to the control and jealously of their new wife or because the men continued to be as badly behaved as they had been here and had only married for a visa to get out of the country. The cultural differences were huge between the Dominican Republic and other countries. The lives of the foreign women was about going to work and coming home and watching the television, many didn't even know their neighbours. For the guys this was not the same woman they had met on holiday who had been drinking and dancing. There was no fun, no dancing, no driving with a beer in your hand. Many of the women did not understand the Dominican culture at all, having only spent a few weeks on holiday each year with their now husband, and all of that time was spent on a resort. Very few spoke Spanish and the men only spoke limited English, which led to communication problems as well. The women would write to me asking for advice.

"I want to be number one in his life, but he talks to his mother every day," they would moan.

"Well, I don't think Dominican men do numbers," I would reply. "But if they did then their mother would always be number one."

"That's just wrong," they would complain. "I won't put up with that."

Given there are so few pensions here, all Dominican children are brought up knowing that once they start work they have to give money to their parents, and, indeed, one of the reasons for going overseas, far from friends and family, is to earn more money to give to their families – something else which rarely went down well with foreign wives.

There were successful relationships of course, usually where both spoke each other's language, where they had spent a significant amount of time together off a resort before marrying and where the women understood the culture well. In addition, these couples had discussed issues such as how much money to send back to the family before they married and also how their money would be managed once they did marry.

For those who moved here to be with their Dominican man, sometimes it worked out, but some would slowly be destroyed emotionally and financially over time. To be fair, it was not only women with Dominican men who ended up in that situation, but also many expats living in the country, especially when one partner died or left and they were left on their own. Many of the expats ended up slowly slithering down a slippery slope, trying to survive on very little money. The Dominican Republic takes no prisoners and for every person who was happy and content here there were more who were slowly eaten up not having enough money to survive and with nowhere else to go. Over time many of my expat friends died, Rocky from Rocky

Blues Bar in Sosua, who fixed all my computers, Grahame, the partner of my best friend Ginnie, who had died when we lived in Juan Dolio and many more.

Apart from the DR Sisterhood, I was still working on marketing, *What about Your Saucepans?* and I set off on the bus to Santo Domingo to meet with a book club who had invited me to speak at their monthly meeting. At the same time I was going to hand in my papers to become a Dominican Citizen. I had residency, but it was becoming more and more expensive to renew – around US$1,000 – and if I were a citizen it meant I could vote for Danilo plus there was no renewal every couple of years, so it made sense. The first stage was to hand in a ream of papers and I had them all ready to go for the day after the book club meeting.

Laura met me off the bus.

"Hi Laura, great to meet you," I said, stretching after five hours in a cramped bus.

"So pleased you can come, the ladies are so excited to meet you!" she replied. "Let's go to the apartment where they're all waiting."

We set off driving through Santo Domingo crazy traffic and I was just thinking about eating real food as in the *campo* we were so limited. Maybe I could have a burger, or ribs, or anything but rice and chicken.

"Err... and food," I eventually asked, cautiously.

"Oh, the food is great," replied Laura, navigating from lane to lane. "We always bring food depending on where the book is based."

"My book is based in the Dominican Republic," I said, with my heart sinking.

"Yes, amazing. So we will have Dominican food! Isn't that great?" she said smiling.

"Awesome," I replied, with a fixed grin on my face.

Having said that, it was not rice and beans and was really delicious. We went to a beautiful apartment for the meeting and around twenty ladies came, all of whom had read the book. I had not realised there were so many bright expat ladies working in the capital. Some worked for NGOs, some for private companies and they had been here for varying amounts of time – from a few months to decades. A type of expat I had not met before and I really enjoyed talking to all of them.

Next morning, bright and early, I was off to meet with the lady who translated my birth certificate for me, Olga, who I met when she contacted me having read my blog. The easiest way to describe Olga is that she is a raving nutter. Very, very bright, totally crazy, she is a fifty-something-year-old Dominican legal translator, who lives alone in a cluttered apartment with books all over the place, her Chihuahua called Tsunami, and her cat. She does a fabulous job and having met at her apartment we set off for the *Procuraduria* – the place where you get everything legalized – to get the translation formalized as all translations of legal documents have to be legalized and stamped. Olga went into the *Procuraduria*, which was full of people, grabbed a ticket for our turn and then we went round the corner to the bank to pay the RD$330 fee, then back to the office. She found a man she knew working there and within no time at all we had the stamp and then it was off to the Ministry of Interior and Police who are located in a building called the *Huacalito* – once the biggest building in the country. A *Huacal* is a plastic crate where bottles are kept. The word for bottle is *botella*. *Botella* is also the word for those on the government payroll who don't actually work, and they say there are more people with *botellas* supposedly working in the *Huacalito*, or not as the case may be.

So, there we were at the Ministry. Olga suddenly said in her faultless English, "Lindsay, you're wearing flip flops. You can't wear open shoes in a government building! I'll need to come up with a plan." I was sure, knowing Olga, she would come up with some cunning plan and so we waited for the lift. Olga saw some caterers with cool boxes and trays of food arrive by the lift, and she nodded knowingly at me. I had no idea what she was up to, but I followed her and the caterers into the lift, feeling a bit like a spy.

Olga started talking to the caterers and as the lift approached the thirteenth floor, she handed me a tray of pineapple and she grabbed the cool box. We got out of the lift, behind the caterers, and breezed past the security guards, who had no time to look at my feet, before giving the food and the box back to the caterers. Olga beamed at me. Her cunning plan had worked.

We went into the immigration office and I handed over all my papers: letter asking for citizenship; copy of our marriage certificate and Danilo's birth certificate; colour copy of my passport and Danilo's *cedula*; application form; receipt from the newspaper for an advert announcing my citizenship, four photos and my birth certificate, duly apostilled by the UK foreign office and translated by Olga then legally stamped. The apostille has to be done on any documents which come from overseas, as long as that country is part of The Hague convention, and has to be done in the country where the document was issued. My mum had to get a copy of my birth certificate and get it apostilled, then send it to me. She did it twice as I didn't realise it had to be handed in within six months of the date on the apostille.

"There is a problem," frowned the young immigration clerk. "The name on your marriage certificate is not the same as the name on your birth certificate."

"Well no, as I was married before," I said, pulling out my previous marriage certificate and divorce certificate.

"I need your original marriage certificate and divorce certificate, apostilled and translated,"

"But I could not have married Danilo without these," I said. "They were accepted by the judge who married us, and by Immigration for my residency, so why on earth do you need them again?" He would not be persuaded as most Dominican officials have been to Jobsworth University, so I had to ask mum to get me apostilled copies and send them to Olga to be translated.

We left, somewhat disheartened, and made our way to Wendy's to eat hamburgers and meet a lady who had asked me to speak about *What About Your Saucepans?* at the Santo Domingo International Women's Club. Olga had a discussion with Wendy's management on how to improve customer service and stop queue jumping and how to treat elderly customers, handing out her business cards to everyone in the place. Then I left to get the bus back to the *campo*.

Miguel was a neighbour, married to Barbara, or, as they say their names here – Baybara and he is Migay. Miguel was always working. He had a piece of land about a quarter of a mile away, an allotment or, as they say in Spanish, a *conuco*. He would go there most days on his motorcycle carrying a myriad of plastic containers of water and look after his peas and yuca. A couple of months ago he was feeling breathless and woke in the night unable to breathe. They took him to hospital where he stayed for a couple of days and was then sent home. The same thing happened again the day he was sent home, so he went back to hospital and after a few more days had a chest x-ray and an ECG. They sent him home again. I went to see him and checked his pulse, which was racing, over two hundred and fifty beats a minute. Eventually he went back to hospital where the cardiologist diagnosed heart problems and he was sent to a specialist heart hospital in Santo Domingo, the capital. They eventually operated and replaced two heart valves. He stayed with relatives in Santo Domingo until his wound healed and as he and Baybara had been away neighbours were cleaning their house and tidying up the garden. Then they decided to build him a bathroom. The dream of most *campo* folk is to have a real bathroom and few do. Instead, they have a latrine at the bottom of the garden. As latrines go, Miguel and Barbara had a nice one, painted green and with a roof as well. They also used it to store the chicken food.

I don't have a particular problem using latrines. When I was growing up we lived in a caravan and had a chemical toilet called an Elsan. Unlike latrines here where the hole seems pretty deep, the Elson was just like a big bucket and you had to put a blue liquid in it. I remember hating having to go to the toilet when it got full as if you did a number two, as mother would call it, your bottom got splashed. The Elson man would come every Thursday to empty it – we called him Dan Dan the Elson man – and he had a little old van with a bigger tank in it, and he would just pour the contents of our Elson into his bigger tank. Anyway, I digress.

As well as a latrine, Miguel and Barbara had a shower room. Well, it was a few pieces of zinc sheeting stuck onto the outside of the house with a bucket inside and a tin can for scooping the water out of the bucket.

So now the neighbours began to build Miguel a proper bathroom, which was stuck onto the bedroom at the side. It was made of concrete block rather than wood like the rest of the house. I am not sure why that is, but all the bathrooms people build in the *campos*, usually using money from their kids, are made from concrete block. It seems to be the dream of most of the children – to build their parents a bathroom.

I continued with my quest to become Dominican. Mother got a copy of my first marriage certificate and my divorce certificate and sent them to be apostilled. She sent them here using DHL and I then scanned them to Olga to translate and a week later I set off again to get it legalized at the *Procuraduria* and then to hand them in. Going to Santo Domingo was a pain as it meant getting to the local town, Mao, and then catching a bus for the five-hour journey to the capital. Then five hours back again. The buses were comfortable enough, even had a toilet, but usually freezing cold as the air con was on maximum and every so often they crashed, so Danilo would tell me to sit behind the driver as the driver did not want to die so would crash the bus on the other side. I always took his advice.

This time I expected no problems, but it was not to be. There were a thousand people at the *Procuraduria* waiting for documents to be legalized, so Olga in her inimitable fashion chatted to her mate there who said we could queue jump, and we went off to the bank to pay for the stamp. The system was down. BanReservas said the *Procuraduria* system was down and the *Procuraduria* said the bank system was. Whatever. Outside the bank were hundreds waiting to pay and no one knew how long whoever's system it was would be down for, and whether it would be hours or days. It was obvious there was no way anything would be stamped that day as you had to pay the fee for the stamp before you got it. Off to the Ministry of Interior and Police to check whether Olga could hand in the papers for me –which she could. Why didn't I think of that earlier? Olga went two days later, handed in the papers and all were accepted.

Although the interview is supposed to be two weeks after you hand in your papers, my date was two months away in early April, 2015. Dominican two weeks. But at least I was getting there, albeit slowly. I returned to the *campo* the same day.

At this time we had lots of dogs. We still had Meg, the grumpy Chow/ Rottweiler cross, Belinda the Great Dane and Lobo the Husky. We also had two twelve-month-old puppies, Panda and Pandora, who were the son and daughter of Meg and Lobo. As there were no vets at all in the area I always tried to keep them apart when the females were on heat, but Danilo invariably left the door open and one would escape. Panda and Pandora were adorable. Long haired, always running around and playing, they would spend the evenings curled up with me on the couch watching television. Every morning they would go scampering and running through the woods and return bang on noon for lunch. We tried to keep them in by fencing off the front garden, but they would dig holes under the fence, and when we blocked it all off using concrete blocks, Pandora would jump the six foot fence and work on one side while Panda worked on the other and between them they would escape.

There was no problem with them running free as they always came back, but the issue was they chased and killed chickens. That is a 'no no' in the *campo*.

This particular day they left before dawn and when noon arrived they were not back.

"Danilo, I'm worried about the Pandas. They're always back for lunch," I said to him. "Where are they? What's happened to them?"

"They be back soon," he said confidently.

"Well, go and call them as they will hear your voice, and mine isn't strong enough," I ordered.

He yelled, "*Perrote, perro nudo, perrote!!*" This was Danilo speak, which is what he always called the dogs. I have no idea what it means but *perro* means dog and *nudo* is a knot and he says the dogs tie us up in knots

Nothing and no sign. I walked up and down the garden all afternoon, leaning over the fence into the woods, calling them. Danilo went further afield looking for them and no sign. That night I could hardly sleep hoping I would hear them barking at the back door. There was just silence.

The following day Danilo went off looking for them in the car and asking people if they had seen them. I knew something bad had happened, but I hoped maybe they had killed a chicken and the owner of the chicken had locked them up until we found them and paid for the chicken. Danilo asked everyone he could and offered money to anyone who could find them, but still nothing.

The next day, he came home looking sombre.

"I have found them. They is dead. They kill a prize cockerel who has a General. The General he say poison them, and the worker he put down meat with *la nata* and they die very quick. "

"What is *la nata*," I asked, feeling numb even though I had known they were not coming back. Danilo explained that it was a very powerful poison made from caterpillars, which the Taíno Indians used to put on the tips of their spears and arrows. They ate the meat and died almost instantly.

Danilo spoke to the poisoner and he apologised, but he had to do what the General said. He buried the dogs where they had died, next to each other, in their favourite woods. My only solace was that in their twelve months on this earth they had had a fantastic life, running through the woods. I had never known such happy dogs. I missed them terribly and that all too familiar ache in my chest, which I last had when Tyson died, came back with a vengeance.

Danilo always had plans apart from his political ambitions. His latest was that we were going to breed turkeys and then sell them at Christmas time and become millionaires. He turned up with three turkeys who we named Stuffing, who was the male, and two females, Sprout and Parsnip, or as Danilo called them, Etuffin, Esprow and Parnees.

Turkeys are most peculiar birds. Stuffing kept puffing himself up and doing a funny little walk and sticking his tail in the air while changing his face at the same time. One minute it was blue and white and then this thing on his nose, which was usually a white stub about an inch long, would turn red and dangle down about six inches. Apparently it was called a snood and served no useful purpose, but was there to attract the female as was his red wrinkly neck, which was called the wattle. In Spanish the word for the snood is *moco*, which also means snot. They both filled with blood and turned red when he was aroused, which in Stuffing's case was every five minutes it seemed.

The turkeys were loose in the back garden, but we had only had them a couple of days when night began to fall and Parsnip decided to roost on the fence round the doghouse. It took Lobo seconds to knock her off her perch and set on her. I managed to get him off and although she had a hole either side of her chest she made a miraculous recovery.

If they were intelligent, which I understood turkeys were not, they would be able to take themselves off to bed, but when they were loose Danilo had to pick them up and put them on their perches in the cellar. Given I wouldn't do that when Danilo was away playing at mayor in Guayacanes, he had to put them back under the balcony and they stayed there day and night.

Angela came to the gate.

"Lindsay, Leida's had a stroke. They're sending her home from hospital as there's nothing they can do."

Leida was the lady with one leg and diabetes who lived with her husband who owned the *colmado*, Sukin. They lived next to Barbara and Miguel, who had returned from his successful heart surgery. As is usual here, when the hospital realised they could do nothing they sent her home so that, I was told, "God could decide."

"Her children are coming from New York," continued Angela.

"Well, I hope they are prepared for a long wait," I said. "People don't always die quickly from strokes and she may even recover."

"I don't think her children can come for long," replied Angela. "They only have a couple of days off work."

"The injection?" I asked. Angela just looked at me knowingly.

Leida never regained consciousness and family and friends looked after her and fed her through a feeding tube in her nose. Her children arrived from New York and almost immediately the doctor was called and put up a drip, and, just like Lala, she died about thirty minutes later.

The funeral was arranged very quickly. She died at three in the afternoon and by four o'clock she was washed, dressed, made up and in her coffin. As is usual here, the coffin was left open on the dining room table and placed on large blocks of ice. The house filled up and everyone stayed up all night, although I made my excuses after a couple of hours. There must have been around a hundred people in the house and garden with cups of coffee to keep everyone awake. In the morning the hearse arrived and we drove very slowly to the church, some cars, motorcycles, and many people walking.

The church was the local Catholic church and it was full to bursting. For some reason, whenever I am in church here, I always remember that I am in the Caribbean. The fans were all on overhead, under the corrugated zinc roof, and making that squeaking sound that overhead fans often do. The windows had wooden slats in them so there were stripes of sunlight throughout the church, across the wooden pews. Her coffin was open, in the middle of the church, and the breeze from the fans was blowing the white silk frill, as well as her hair. The service was about an hour long and the priest invited everyone to go and visit the coffin to say their last goodbyes, and, again, as is the custom, all the smart phones came out as people took their last photo of her. Many non-Dominicans say to me how awful it is that people see the dead and take photographs, but if you explain to a Dominican how we deal with death, they are appalled at the fact the family do not usually wash the body and even more appalled that the dead are kept in a deep freeze for a while before burial. If you mention cremation, hands get thrown up in the air in horror.

We then had another slow journey to the cemetery, which was around a mile away down a dusty narrow steep track, surrounded by sugar cane fields. By now it was noon, and very, very hot. The coffin was unloaded and she was viewed for the last time. I was surprised no one was smashing the coffin to bits with axes and machetes, which is what usually happens to nice coffins so that no one steals it. The reason soon became clear as the coffin was placed in a breeze block box which had been built above ground, plywood was placed on the top and then two men mixed up cement on the ground next to the coffin and shovelled it in on top. No way could anyone steal that coffin.

We had to wait in the boiling heat with no shade until the job was completed, which took around an hour, then home for a late lunch.

Following Miguel's heart surgery and Leida's death I thought the *campo* had had enough trauma and sadness, but unfortunately it carried on. Barbara was diagnosed with cancer – multiple myeloma, although she didn't actually know what it was as the family didn't want to tell her. I had never heard of this cancer, but it really is horrid and affects the plasma in the bone marrow. The upshot was that she was very anaemic, had bone pain and then kidney failure. The treatment is chemo, but the cost was US$4,000 a month, which the insurance company wouldn't pay and no way could anyone raise that amount once, let alone for the eight months she needed it. She moved to Santiago to stay with her daughter near the hospital and had dialysis twice a week. She lost an awful amount of weight and the family was just trusting in God that she would recover. She came home around once a month, and each time I saw her she looked worse. It was only a matter of time for this amazing person, who had been so good to us and who really was the life and soul of the *campo*.

At the same time another neighbour, Leopoldo, husband of Angela the *bruja*, not even fifty, had a brain tumour. Apparently it was benign but growing and he had already lost most of the vision in his left eye. He was battling with the insurance company to raise the money to have it removed, at a cost of around US$14,000. It seemed so unfair all of these neighbours being so sick and unable to have the life saving treatment they needed.

It was time for my annual few days off. I was writing articles for *International Living Magazine*, which usually involved interviewing expats. One of them was to be an American called Dan, living in Las Terrenas, a beach town in the north-east corner of the country and somewhere I had never been. Dan and his Dominican wife, Manty, had some apartments for rent as holiday lets and he suggested I go and stay with them for a couple of nights and I could also interview him at the same time, so I decided to go with my best friend, Chivirico.

It was a long way to Las Terrenas and the first part of the journey was to catch a bus to Santiago, which took around an hour. The bus dropped us off close to the bus stop for Las Terrenas and Chivirico was in charge asking people where it was. There were three buses a day – 6am, 11.30am and 3pm. We caught the 11.30am and I was pleasantly surprised that although it was a mini bus, it was comfortable, air conditioned and had free wifi. Chivirico grabbed my phone and was busy chatting to Danilo and his aunt Ana on Whatsapp – something I had no idea how to use, and I was amazed that a seven-year-old knew more than I did.

The journey to Las Terrenas took around four hours with a stop in San Francisco de Macoris for food and the toilets. As is usual on the buses here everyone shared their food, chatted and sang along to the music. Every so often the bus stopped and picked up a guy selling cheese, or sweets or sunglasses and they made a few sales and hopped off the bus again.

Eventually we reached Sanchez, which is on the southern coast of the Samana peninsula and drove north over the mountain, with stunning views, into Las Terrenas, which lies on the Atlantic north coast.

"You can see the sea De Fe," exclaimed Chivirico, having woken up. "Look at that sea, wow!" and he started jumping up and down in his seat. It was not what I expected. On first impressions Las Terrenas was like Sosúa and Cabarete on the north coast, which are both tourist towns with lots of touristy type shops, but if you looked closely there were everyday

Dominican shops interspersed such as a cobbler, banks, *colmados* and hardware stores. I also spotted a French bakery, which I made a vow to check out.

Dan and Manty's guesthouse was easy to spot. A massive sign right opposite one of the plazas – Plaza Kanesh in the main street – and grey haired Dan stood there grinning at us in front of the sign. Chivirico ran to meet him and gave him a hug, immediately making another friend for life.

From there it was only around a fifty-yard walk to the guesthouse, which was like being in another world. It was a large piece of land where Dan and Manty lived, as did many of Manty's brothers and sisters, in little wooden houses scattered throughout the land. Dan and Manty had a larger concrete property and they lived upstairs and downstairs there were three guest rooms each with a bed, outdoor sitting area, kitchen, bathroom and all mod cons including wifi and hot water.

"I'm having this side of the bed," announced Chivirico, putting his pyjamas under the pillow and carrying on unpacking. "I will have this shelf, and you can have the one above as I can't reach it," he continued, and lay all his clothes neatly on the shelf.

Once we had unpacked we went to be introduced to Manty, then Chivirico, Dan and I went off for a twenty-minute walk through the town to the beach. I was surprised there were no people trying to sell us stuff on the street, nor pull us into their shops, and when we reached the beach there were no beach sellers. Somehow the place had a different ambiance than other Dominican resort towns I had been to. It felt more European and more chic. The number of motorbikes and quad bikes was amazing and they were all tearing through the town and along the beach road.

I had no idea there were so many beaches in Las Terrenas and no idea the beaches were so nice and clean and the sea was amazing. Chivirico was in his element swimming in the ocean with Dan or doing the obligatory covering himself with sand.

The following day we discovered the French supermarket, full of things I had not seen for years such as rice noodles, Thai spices, mushrooms, amazing cheeses and the biggest wine selection I had ever seen.

"I need to cook my coconut biscuits for Manty," exclaimed Chivirico, as he marched around the supermarket grabbing flour, sugar and desiccated coconut. We dumped our shopping back in our room and went back down to the beach. On the way Chivirico bought himself a snorkel and mask and planned to catch fish. No fish were caught, but he still had great fun with Dan in the water. In the evening Manty cooked and once we had eaten Chiv sat using my computer to listen to music videos, and I sat chatting with Dan over a glass of rum. It was lovely to talk in English and hear about his journey, how he came to the Dominican Republic and his plans for the future. His idea was to convert more of the house into a backpackers' hostel, with a central living area and dormitories. I had no idea there were so many backpackers in the Dominican Republic, but it seemed like a good idea and within no time at all they were number one on Trip Advisor.

The next day Chivirico and I set off for Mojitos, which was a bar on the beach at Punta Poppy. I had written about Mojitos in various travel books so I was keen to see it for myself. I cannot think of a better way to spend a day on the beach than with food and drink within easy reach, beach chairs and shade. Chivirico spent the day in the ocean with me keeping a careful eye on him and we ordered lunch.

"What do you want Chiv?" I asked. "There's a special menu for children," I pointed out to him.

"Fish fingers and chips," he replied. "But fish don't have fingers."

"They are shaped like fingers, but made of fish," I explained.

"Is there ketchup? "

"Yes, there will be ketchup."

"Okay," he yelled, as he ran back into the ocean.

I was taking advantage of the wifi in the bar when a lady approached me.

"Excuse me, but are you Lindsay de Feliz?" she asked.

"Yes, that's me," I replied, somewhat confused.

"Oh my God. I've read your book!" she exclaimed. "I loved it, I can't believe I'm meeting you!" and she sat down at the table next to me. The lady was a fellow Brit called Helen and she and her husband and business partner Doug ran a real estate company and a building and property services company in Las Terrenas. We had a great time chatting and she then took Chivirico and me to yet another beach, even more beautiful – Las Ballenas. On the way there we passed the famous fishermen's village, which burned down a few years ago, but now has been rebuilt. A lovely row of charming wooden buildings mostly used as bars and restaurants, overlooking the ocean.

We ate with Dan and Manty again that evening and, after dinner, Chivirico cooked his famous coconut biscuits.

All too soon it was time to come home. We caught the bus back to Santiago at 6am buying fresh *pain au chocolat* from the French bakery for the journey, which was open even at that time in the morning. By noon we were back home.

So. Las Terrenas. I thought it was small – it isn't, the population is over four thousand. I thought it was full of French people – the only French accent I heard was the baker in the French bakery. I am sure they are there, but I didn't see them. I did see and meet a whole range of other nationalities. I didn't see the usual expat drinking at the bar. All the expats I met were working, most with their own businesses. The beaches were much better than I imagined, as were the shops and facilities. I thought it was a long way away from everywhere, but with all of the new roads it is only now two hours from Santo Domingo, and there are five buses a day, and four hours from Santiago with three buses a day. I thought it would be expensive, but it wasn't as bad as I thought. I had no idea there were so many backpackers in the area, and talking to them they were all travelling round the country and the Dominican Republic is now a popular place for backpackers with hostels opening up all over the country.

I realised as I was walking around that it really is important for those who want to settle here to visit the whole country before making a decision on where to live, as had I visited Las Terrenas before, I am sure it would have made it to the top of my list as a place I wanted to live.

CHAPTER SEVEN
BACK TO POLITICS

"But do not distress yourself with dark imaginings.
Many fears are born of fatigue and loneliness."
Desiderata, Max Ehrmann 1927

DANILO WAS MORE AND MORE INVOLVED IN POLITICS AND
spending every other weekend back in Guayacanes. He was
once again running for the Dominican Liberation Party, or
PLD, the same party as before. The purple party. During the
2010 elections the official colour of the main opposition party
– the Dominican Revolutionary Party or PRD – was white. That
was the party of the current mayor of Guayacanes. However,
the PRD had been fighting internally, often literally shooting

each other, and divided into two during the intervening years so we now also had the PRM or the Modern Revolutionary Party, who's official colour was also white.

The President, Danilo Medina was PLD, the head of the PRD was a chap called Miguel Vargas, and the head of the PRM was a guy called Luis Abinader.

The PLD president before Medina was Leonel Fernandez and he was unable to run as the constitution said you could only run for one term and not subsequent ones, which was why Medina ran and won. No one expected great things of him as he appeared to be a quiet and introspective man. He was short, wore glasses and did not appear to have a magnetic personality. But everyone was surprised as he gave 4% of the GDP to education for the first time and transformed the system to allow everyone to go to school from nine to four rather than just mornings or afternoons. New schools were built around the country, teachers' training was improved and their salaries rose dramatically. Nursery schools were built around the country too, as well as a continued programme of road improvements. He began to make surprise visits into the countryside every Sunday, visiting small farmers and providing them with low interest loans to improve production. Unemployment fell and tourism grew and his popularity ratings went through the roof.

People were clamouring for him to run again, but according to the constitution he could not. It appeared the deal was he could be president for one term and then Leonel would run again. But not only did people want Danilo to run again, they didn't want Leonel so there was a chance the party would lose if he ran. There was only one thing for it – change the Constitution to allow him to run again. However, there was one minor technical hitch in that he would not be able to get the number of congress votes needed, which was two thirds, as obviously all of the opposition members would oppose him standing again, knowing he would win. Simple answer to that one – do a deal. Which is what he did. He did a deal with the main opposition party, the PRD, and promised Miguel Vargas a good job, and that in each of the municipalities there would only be one candidate – either PRD or PLD but not both. Part of their deal was that where existing positions of Deputy, Senator and Mayor were held by PRD people, the PLD would not field a candidate against them.

As happened in our case. The case of Guayacanes. My Danilo, as opposed to the president, had been working for a year and was top of the polls, but the existing mayor, John Hazim, was PRD so it looked like Danilo would not be able to stand as there could only be one candidate from the PLD/ PRD alliance.

This was a bit of a blow, as by then all of the posters were printed, his campaign office was set up and painted purple, and he had great support from the PLD people and members in the municipality.

It was then decided that in those municipalities where there was a candidate from each party – PLD and PRD – there would be an opinion poll, and whoever won would be the candidate.

"That is very good for me, as I win easy," said Danilo confidently, as we were discussing the situation over lunch. "No problem for me, as no one like other man. I win."

It was clear he would win, as we had carried out several polls and he was always well in the lead with around 70% of the votes, and even official polls were saying the same. We kept having calls saying they were polling this weekend and then again and again and each time he had to rush back to Guayacanes to make sure he was seen and was in front of everyone's mind.

We got to the stage where they had done opinion polls and said that whoever had the highest with a margin of 10% would be the candidate. Danilo had over 50% and the existing mayor had 9%. Every other place in the country was announced – apart from Guayacanes. It appeared they would give it to the existing mayor, and the party – PLD – said they would offer Danilo a job. Which they didn't, what a surprise, so he signed up to be the candidate for another party. This other party was called the PLR – *Partido Liberal Reformista*, and the guy who owned/ ran it was a chap called Amable Aristy. *Amable* means friendly so we had Mr. Happy (Danilo, as Feliz, his surname, meant happy) going with Mr. Friendly. Mr. Friendly was into helping people so it seemed a good fit. However, the PLD was purple and this new one was yellow and green so Danilo had a week to change all his posters to yellow and green and repaint his campaign headquarters, and change the PLD star to the PLR sunflower.

Meanwhile, I was getting used to being alone most evenings as Danilo was at university until 10pm or later, and away a few days each week. It wasn't just a question of getting up, grabbing a coffee and sitting down at my computer for the day, there was a lot to be done. There were the dogs to be fed at noon – by now we had two more puppies as Danilo had let Meg out again. These two were *Grita Mucho*, which means 'scream a lot' as she did, and Sweepy, her brother, who looked like a big black furry husky.

My plan to have one chicken lay one egg a day had gone horribly wrong and while we had chickens and a cockerel in the hen house at the front of the house, in the back garden we had more chickens roaming free and a massive rooster we called Monster, who weighed over twenty pounds. He had taken up with the turkeys, by now there was Stuffing and Sprout and one baby turkey. The plan of breeding on a massive scale did not really work – although Sprout sat on her clutch of eggs she only produced one baby. Parsnip, who was supposed to be a female turned out to be a male, so he had to go as he was fighting with Stuffing. My job was to feed the chickens and the turkeys and make sure the dogs didn't get at them. Stuffing and Monster slept in the fenced off area under the balcony – there was a hole in the front so they could go in and out – and Sprout and chick and Cranberry in the cellar. They would wander around in the day and had learned to take themselves off to bed at night.

Belinda and Meg were on heat so they were in the house and not allowed out the front and Lobo and the puppies were out the front or in the doghouse. I would take Meg and Belinda into the back garden for a toilet trip a couple of times a day and they were fine with Monster and the turkeys. However, this one night it had been raining although now was only spitting and I took them down the steps from the living room into the garden.

Stuffing had been sick for a couple of weeks, not eating much, so Danilo was force-feeding him, but Stuffing was also depressed. Unbeknown to me, this particular night, Stuffing had not gone to bed and was lurking outside his pen when I took the dogs out for their nightly poo and pee trip. Suddenly, for some unknown reason the dogs went for him. As it was dark I couldn't see him, but I heard him screaming, shone the torch and saw the dogs attacking him. I desperately tried to get the dogs off him, hitting them on their noses with the torch. I was covered in mud, rolling on the ground smacking the dogs trying to make them let go of Stuffing while I tried to hold Stuffing to protect him. There was a bougainvillea right there and I had scratches on my face and arms as we were all flailing around in the mud. In the end the dogs let go and I pulled Stuffing into the area under the balcony. He was dead, but I thought if Danilo saw him dead in his house he would think he died of his illness and the dogs wouldn't get into trouble. I came inside, shaking, cut, bleeding, covered in my blood and Stuffing's blood, and filthy. I slumped down on the tiled floor, shaking like a leaf and, when at last I calmed down, which took a while, I went upstairs and had a hot shower before crawling into bed.

I woke up when Danilo returned and heard him go into the back garden, so once he came upstairs into the bedroom I sleepily said,

"It's sad about Stuffing, but he had been ill."

"The dogs kill Etuffy," replied Danilo.

"No they didn't," I said. "Why would you say that?"

"Etuffy head not estuck on his body, that is why," answered Danilo. "If dogs no kill him how do head fall off?"

Bit of a giveaway that. RIP Stuffing.

And it wasn't just Stuffing who went to meet his maker.

Sukin, the owner of the *colmado*, whose wife, Leida died four months previously, also died. Since Leida died, he had not been living alone as apparently men cannot live on their own in the *campo*. A woman came in the daytime to clean and cook for him, and her son came at night and slept in the house. Sukin was fine, he would always be sitting on his front porch rocking slowly in his rocking chair and pulling himself out of it when he had a customer for the *colmado*. Every time I approached, coming in through the gate between his house and Barbara's and Miguel's, he would say, "Ay Lindsay," in his usual weary way and wander with me to the little *colmado* at the end of the garden.

Sometimes, when Danilo was at university at night, I would pop round to see him and Miguel, both alone and we would sit companionably chatting until Miguel left to go and stay at a relative's house up the road.

Sukin decided he needed a break and went to visit his sister in Santiago for a fortnight. He simply never came back. Apparently he had a stroke, ended up in a coma on a ventilator then I assume was switched off. So his house was empty and the *colmado* closed.

I now had to walk about fifteen minutes to another *colmado*, rather than having one fifty yards away, but they did stock a lot more than Sukin.

As well as Sukin and Stuffing dying, everyone's chickens were dying as well. No one knows why, although some said it was the changing of the seasons from summer to winter. I keep asking the locals to try and get to the bottom of it, and they said the chickens didn't actually die, they went to sleep at night and didn't wake up. Sprout and Cranberry both died too, they went to sleep and didn't wake up, which put an end to Danilo's money spinning idea number sixty-two. I waited with bated breath to hear the next one.

The puppies, Sweepy and *Grita Mucho* grew like topsy and caused total havoc – eating the furniture, chasing chickens and annoying Belinda. Several months ago a man borrowed Lobo's bits and brought his long-haired Alsatian bitch to mate with him. Lobo performed splendidly and the dog was pregnant. We were promised one of the litter. Well, the man sold the litter and Danilo told him he was not allowed to borrow Lobo again. Next thing we knew he delivered a dog, supposedly the son of Meg and Lobo's daughter (who he took from the litter) and a Belgian Shepherd. Now this dog was the size of a Chihuahua when he arrived and I was all for sending him back. However, he was cute and eventually grew into a massive, well-mannered and good looking dog who lived with Lobo and Sweepy in the doghouse. He was called Rin Tin Tin as he had big ears.

Danilo was spending more and more time in Guayacanes and had taken leave of absence from university to concentrate of becoming mayor. Life without him and living alone in the *campo* was anything but easy and I began to start to feel the effects of the stress. It was also lonely as our vibrant little *campo* had been decimated with the loss of Sukin and Leida, and Barbara was in Santiago. I had no car as Danilo had driven it while his was off the road and the result of him only driving it in first and second gear was that the pistons broke and we did not have the money to get it fixed. This meant I had no transport. Basic stuff I could get from the *colmado*, a fifteen minute walk away, but anything more than basic, such as vegetables or bacon or sliced bread or juice, I had to walk to the village shop which was around a mile and a half away. It was fine walking there, but hard work walking back especially laden down with vegetables, although sometimes I did manage to get a lift back.

Some things were a little more difficult, such as buying sacks of dog food, which meant getting a bus into town that took around thirty minutes once the bus came, although there was only one every hour and it was often full, so you had to wait for the next one or hope someone would give you a lift. Once in town I had to walk to the pet food store, and then hop on a *motoconcho* taxi to take me, and the massive bag of food, to the bus stop to come home. The bus driver would load the dog food onto the bus then drop me off on the road near the house and I would wait for someone to appear who could help me carry the fifty pound sack home. I didn't usually have to wait long.

Daily life was hard alone. I had no one to kill tarantulas, poisonous centipedes, scorpions. No one to chase the bats out, which flew into the bedroom at night, or get rid of the massive moths which looked like pterodactyls. No one to get rid of snakes or dead chickens.

I went outside to feed the chickens one day and no sign of Monster, so I looked in the cellar where he had moved after Stuffing was murdered as one assumes he did not want to lose his head either, and he was lying in there – dead. I really could not deal with dead animals for some reason and given the size of Monster there was no way I could scoop him into a plastic bag without touching him. When the dogs killed the neighbours' chickens in the front garden, by using the dustpan – which was on a long stick – and a brush I could usually scoop them into a few plastic bags while muttering to myself *I can't do this, oh my God I can't do this. Yes, you can, just do it. I can't. Oh bloody hell, it's fallen off the dustpan. Just do it woman.* And then yelling, *Oh My God, Oh My God, Oh My God, Oh My God,* once I had the dead, bleeding beast in the plastic bags, running to the dustbin with the bag at arms' length and throwing them in. Around ten minutes later my breathing would return to normal. Around a day or two later they would start to smell.

Every day I would be sitting at the computer then hear the dogs barking and a chicken squealing and would rush outside, armed with a broom, to try and get the dogs off the chicken or hope it had escaped and flown off. The worst situation was if they injured the chicken, which then couldn't fly, but lay there squawking in agony as it was not dead. Then what was I supposed to do? I couldn't scoop a half-dead chicken into a plastic bag and throw it in the bin. I did try once and the bloody thing flew at me sending me into a hysterical frenzy as I was splattered with chicken blood and feathers as it flew at my face. No way would I do that again, so I came up with the cunning plan of putting a bucket on top of them in the short term until I could find someone to help me.

I went around to the neighbours to ask for help with Monster. Given most had died or were ill I was a bit short of help, and every time I asked Berto, who owned the detested fighting cocks and lived behind us, he would say no. I asked for help with a boa constrictor who was in one of the trees, only about ten feet long, but he said no as he was scared of snakes. He was scared of dogs too, so would never come into my garden to help with chicken issues even if the dogs were locked up and the nearest he came was throwing rocks at the dogs when one of his chickens flew over the fence. I did ask him to clip his chickens' wings or keep them in pens, but he refused.

So, I called Angela, the *bruja*.

"Angela, Monster's dead and I just can't bury him. Is there any way you could help me? He needs taking down the garden to the cemetery and burying with Silly Boy, and the dead cats, and the dead turkeys."

"Sure, I'll be there soon. I'm at my mum's in the village so it'll be a few minutes."

True to her word, ten minutes later, Angela turned up on the back of a motorbike and she and motorbike man went round to the cellar, picked up Monster by his massive yellow legs and carried him down the garden as if it was nothing.

"He isn't dead," yelled Angela, as she was halfway down the garden, picking her way carefully between the pumpkins. "He just fell asleep and didn't wake up."

From then on, Angela was my 'go to' person in emergencies and she never let me down.

As night would fall I would chat to people on Facebook, DR Sisterhood people and friends. Every night at 6pm I would chat to Shirley, who was alone in her *finca* and we would go through the traumas of the day. Many people had written to me having read *What about your Saucepans?* which was lovely and some had become friends, especially an American lady called Kate who would talk to me every day and made me laugh. But I was finding it increasingly hard to go to sleep at night. I wasn't really afraid, even though the house was open and had no locks so anyone could come in at any time. I would go up the stairs to bed, but it was all dark upstairs as when the lightning hit us and all of the light bulbs blew, they were so high up that we could not replace the ones in the upstairs hallway, round the upstairs balcony and in the upstairs living room. There was one working in the bedrooms and the bathroom, but I had to feel my way round to the bedroom unless I remembered to take the torch with me.

Belinda and Meg and *Grita Mucho* would come up to bed with me, as I liked the company. None would sleep on the bed, but Meg would sleep next to the bed, Belinda on the sofa in the upstairs living area and *Grita* would spend all night taking things out of the bedroom, destroying them and leaving them on the roof above the front door. It was impossible to keep her out because of the cat holes Danilo made in the upstairs doors and she would just come in through them.

Once I lay in bed I could not sleep and could hear my heart pounding in my chest, so much so it felt as if the whole bed was vibrating. Nothing I could do would make it stop. On the one hand I wanted to take a sleeping pill to sleep, but then what would I do if there was a problem in the middle of the night? All my concerns magnified tenfold once I lay there. Where would I get more money from for the campaign? What should I do about the chickens? How was I going to get all my work done? Nothing worked to get me to sleep and I would spend half the night squatting on the balcony outside the bedroom having a glass of rum and a cigarette to try and calm down and banish these worries from my overactive brain.

The mornings of adoring living here and leaping out of bed were over. I would drag myself up, gritting my teeth at the idea of another day, waiting for the next disaster to strike as every day I was running in and out to rescue neighbours' chickens or our baby chicks who couldn't find their mother or some other problem.

It didn't take long for the next disaster.

I was sitting at my desk working and it sounded like a train was coming. From deep in my memory banks I was suddenly transported back to London and travelling to work on the tube. I could hear the train approaching as it rushed through the tunnel, but the other part of my brain told me there were no trains here. I sat for only seconds trying to process this, then as it sounded like the 'train' was about to ram the house, I stood up to run outside. At the same time, the dogs all ran inside and as I stood up to run out I fell over. The floor was moving, the windows all rattled and all of the bottles and pots and jars fell off the kitchen counters. Pictures fell off the walls as I struggled to my feet. *Shit! Earthquake!* I realised, as I ran outside followed by the dogs. I reached the front door and could not see a thing. There was a massive dust cloud. The whole of the front garden was just dust. Brown gritty dust. I had no idea what to do. Was it over? Would there be aftershocks? Should I go inside again or stay outside? My brain was scrambled. My immediate reaction was to call Danilo as he would know what to do, so I rushed inside and grabbed my phone before running out again and calling him.

"Danilo. Earthquake. *Terremoto*," I gasped.

"How big?" he asked.

"I don't know, I need to check online but should I go back in the house? I don't know what to do," I yelled down the phone.

"Si. No problem. *Terremoto* he gone," he replied calmly.

I walked back, trembling, into the house and began to put things back where they belonged and clean up the mess. When I had finished I checked online and it was 4.6 on the Richter scale, not that strong but the epicentre was only ten miles from me. I called Danilo back.

"It was a 4.6 but very close to here," I explained.

"*Ese no es na*. That she is nothing. Very little erquack."

Well, it certainly was something to me. My first, and I hope my last, earthquake.

Life continued to be pretty stressful with the animals as I had a mother hen, *Coja*, and her baby chicks under the balcony, but the stupid chicks kept escaping through the chicken wire and then they couldn't get back in. So every time I heard frantic cheeping I had to run outside to get them back in, without letting the dogs out in the process. Even worse was when they escaped from under the balcony and went next door into the dog run. I had to distract the dogs, close the dog run, so they couldn't murder the chick, and then put it back.

The other issue was the escaping puppies and it did not matter how many times I blocked up holes in the fence, the little buggers always found a way of digging under the fence, ripping my repairs apart or *Grita Mucho* would simply jump over and I was terrified they would meet the same fate as the Pandas.

I had no money as Danilo had the ATM card to take money out of the bank as and when I earned it or raised it. When I needed cash I would call him and he would send it to me via Western Union and I would get the bus into town to collect it or he would send one of the kids to bring me money and anything else I needed. The money was to pay the electricity, phone and Internet bills and buy chicken and dog food. My food was way down the list as I permanently felt so stressed I had no appetite.

The weight started to fall off me and within a couple of months I was down to eighty pounds.

People would suggest I went home to the UK until the election was over, but that would be anything but simple to do. First, who would look after the animals? Second, my citizenship still was not through even though I had passed the interview and they said it would take four months to finalize. That was a year ago and the Ministry said they were waiting for my Interpol report. This meant, as I had not renewed my residency assuming the citizenship would not take long, I would have to pay a fine when I left the country, which could be up to around £1,000. Also, I could not return into the country without a return ticket to the UK as I had neither Dominican residency nor citizenship, so it was not merely a case of buying a ticket, it was a ticket, plus a return to the UK I would not use, plus the fine. And, however attractive the idea may have been, I didn't want to go. This was my home and I hated the idea of living in England again. What I had to do was to stop myself feeling so stressed, give myself a severe talking to and implement a stress reduction strategy.

The first thing was to stop the dogs getting at the neighbours' chickens and as the neighbours refused to help by locking their chickens up, specifically Berto who only had his fighting cocks in cages, I locked the dogs up and kept them all in the house apart from Lobo in the doghouse, as if he was in the living room he cocked his leg against the furniture. I let them out every couple of hours to go to the toilet, but only after I had scoured the garden first to make sure no chickens were in sight. Apart from that the big metal front door remained closed day and night. Within a couple of days Berto and Feluche were yelling my name to see if I was okay. I explained they had left me no choice but to be locked in the house – not that it seemed to bother them.

The only problem was at meal times as, although the dogs did not usually fight, they had a habit of fighting over food. We used to eat at twelve and then we would feed the dogs, but the idea of feeding them made me too nervous to eat so I had to build up the courage to feed them first and then wait for my nerves to calm down before I ate. I came up with this plan to keep them all apart and in different rooms or parts of the house to eat and that way avoided any of the nasty fights.

It seems ridiculous I was getting in such a state about all of these things, and I really couldn't afford to as I was so busy. I did the Dominican news for DR1 two days a week, Mondays and Tuesdays, I had the work for the American attorneys, I was doing some marketing work for Jonathan who now had a hotel in the Colonial Zone, I had DR Sisterhood clients who I would talk to daily, and more were arriving all the time. I would get emails from people who had read *What about your Saucepans?* which needed replying to, plus constant questions from random people about how things worked in the Dominican Republic. How do I get from A to B? Can I buy this or that medicine in the Dominican Republic? How much will it cost me to rent a flat in X place? Where can I get health insurance from? The list of questions was endless.

On the surface none of my Facebook friends I chatted to daily had any idea how bad things were, nor did the constant stream of DR Sisterhood clients. I was the strong one, the one who could always cope, but as each day passed my nerves were becoming more and more frazzled and doing the simplest of tasks became a major effort.

Danilo knew I was finding it hard to cope, as I would tell him when he called every couple of days. Phone calls were not easy as the only place with a decent signal was in one corner of the upstairs balcony. He would call and I would run upstairs and call him back.

"Danilo, I just can't do this," I would say, hating the fact I sounded so pathetic.

"It isn't for much longer," he would reply. "I be mayor soon then we be back together. I is doing this for us. I want you no work. I want you be First Lady."

Sometimes he would come home for a few days or even just for the night, then I could instantly find myself relaxing and returning to my old self. Unfortunately, it was never for long and the moment he left the black clouds would descend again and nothing I could do would make them lift.

And then came the bees.

I was sitting at the computer, sucking crisps in the vain hope that the dogs would not come rushing to have some once they heard them being crunched, as they were all lying in various spots in the living room apart from Lobo in the doghouse. I was working hard trying to get blogs finished for the American guy I wrote articles for when I heard a buzzing noise. It wasn't just the sound of a fly, it was a very loud buzzing noise following by a crash and then an even louder buzzing noise. I stood up to investigate and saw hordes of bees – literally hundreds of them – flying into the living room through the bars in the doghouse. As I looked through the door there was this massive black mass of what looked like soil, but covered with bees in the middle of the doghouse and I could hardly see Lobo through the curtains of little black buzzing bees. *What on earth is going on?* I had to think quickly to get Lobo away from the bees and stop the bees getting into the house. I opened the door to the doghouse and let Lobo into the main house, and frantically pulled curtains over the doghouse door and ran around shutting the other windows on that side of the house. To no avail as there were already around a hundred bees in the house. Grabbing my phone I rushed outside slamming the door behind me, praying I would get a signal there and called Angela.

"Angela, my house is full of bees! I have no idea what to do."

"On my way," she answered brusquely. "I can cope with bees."

I thought I could, but this was ridiculous.

I ran to the bottom of the front garden making sure the front door was closed so the dogs couldn't get out and I perched on the bench, which was part of the gym, and waited for Angela. You could hardly see the front of the house; it was covered with bees. I looked up and saw a hole in the roof above the doghouse, so it looked like there was some sort of bee mass there, which had fallen down into the doghouse. I daren't move, as although I was only a little allergic to bees, in that a sting would swell up a lot and last ages, I didn't think I could survive hundreds of stings and there was no way of knowing if these were stingy bees or friendly bees. *I could do with Winnie the Pooh here*, I thought wryly.

Angela turned up holding a can of fly spray in her hand, which they call *Baygon* here.

She marched in through the metal gate, sliding it back and strode purposefully up to me.

"See, I can sort bees," she announced, coming straight to me holding out the *Baygon*.

"I think not," I replied, as I pointed towards the house.

"Oh my God, where did so many bees come from?" she gasped, and I pointed up towards the roof.

"Up there, I think, but how the hell do we get rid of them?"

"I call bee man," she declared, and grabbed my phone, standing on the gym bench to try and get a better signal.

Ten minutes later bee man arrived on his clapped-out motorbike. He looked like a normal guy to me, nothing like a bee man was supposed to look with protective clothing and funny hat. He walked towards us.

"Those are bees," he announced, so I silently gave him ten out of ten for intelligence.

"I need my equipment and then I need to find the queen," he said, and with that he got back on his motorcycle and drove off.

I had no idea where he lived, where his equipment was, what it was or when he was coming back and I was a tad concerned as it was nearly noon and if Dominicans don't eat at noon they die, so I feared I would be perched on the gym bench for hours. I need not have worried as twenty minutes later bee man appeared with a sort of stove and a puffer and he was wearing a bee man hat. He had brought help with him in the shape of Angela's husband, who had had his brain tumour successfully removed.

They put ladders up to the beehive and puffed away with their bellows and the remaining bees swarmed in the flame tree next to the doghouse. More and more bees joined the swarm at which stage bee man announced he had the queen and then the other bees tumbled into a canvas bag he had and he drove off with a buzzing squirming bag perched behind him on his motorbike. All that was left for me to do was clean up the remains of the beehive in the dog room, let the dogs out and put some antihistamine cream on Lobo's bee-stung nose.

Danilo returned just before Christmas to spend Christmas day with me, albeit with no tree and no presents, and he proudly delivered my car back to me. If you remember it broke down around six months before as the piston broke due to Danilo driving it in second gear for miles – he can only use first and second in a manual car. He can't do the jiggly bit to put it into third. So the local mechanic said RD$30,000 to fix it, which was a fortune, around U$700, which we didn't have.

Danilo announced he had a mechanic to fix it and off it went, but it appeared this mechanic couldn't fix it as he was born after the Jeep was made in 1988. So, Danilo found a man who actually worked with Mitsubishi engines and sent it to him, although every so often this mechanic asked for more money and it ended up costing more. The Jeep returned on Christmas Eve being driven by Saya (number one dwendy) who went to pay the final amount.

When Saya delivered it back I went outside with him to check the Jeep as I had learned to trust no mechanic.

"Saya, where are the windscreen wipers?"

"What windscreen wipers?"

"The ones that wipe the windscreen and appear to have disappeared."

"Oh, well, they are easy to fix," he replied confidently. I opened the bonnet.

"Where is the windscreen wiper motor?"

"It didn't work."

"I know it didn't work, but the guy was supposed to fix it when he fixed the piston."

"Well, I expect he took the wipers off hoping you would forget," he replied helpfully.

I continued to look the car over.

"He was supposed to solder the exhaust. Look, it's just tied on with a piece of wire," I exclaimed.

"Well, it doesn't rattle anymore," Saya said helpfully.

I went back to the engine.

"What is this funny plastic thing?"

"That's the coil."

"No coil I have seen looks like this. What happened to the original coil?"

"It lost itself."

I decided to check the oil level. There was none. Not a drop, not a tiny microscopic bit of oil.

"Saya, there is no oil in the car."

"He changed the oil and the oil filter," Saya said, confidently.

"Does changing the oil mean taking old oil out and putting new oil in?" I asked.

"Well, taking it out. Maybe he forgot to put it back in."

"And you drove it back a hundred and fifty miles with no oil?" I asked, incredulously.

"It ran fine," he replied. "Well, apart from the white smoke."

"What white smoke?"

"Well, he sent his assistant to put fuel in and he put diesel instead of petrol so now the car makes white smoke. But after running for a bit the smoke goes," Saya answered.

So my jeep left needing a piston and came back running but with no proper coil, no windscreen wipers, exhaust held on by wire, white smoke pouring out of it and goodness knows what damage caused with driving so far with no oil. At least I had transport, but once Danilo went back to Guayacanes my nerves were even more on edge each time I drove it.

CHAPTER EIGHT
ANOTHER ELECTION OVER

*"Exercise caution in your business affairs, for the world
is full of trickery. But let this not blind you to what
virtue there is; many persons strive for high ideals;
and everywhere life is full of heroism."*
Desiderata, Max Ehrmann 1927

IT WAS LOVELY TO HAVE DANILO HOME FOR A FEW DAYS AND I
calmed down, but too soon off he went again and I was back
to my solo life. Before he left I told him I was worried about
Belinda as she seemed to find it hard to breathe and on further
investigation – me and Mr. Google – it appeared she was
suffering from congestive heart failure, which can be common

in Great Danes. There was nothing that could be done about it, apart from give her diuretics, which I did, which seemed to make her breathing easier. To be honest, apart from the fast breathing and fast heartbeat when she was resting, she seemed fine, although I was dreading what might happen as the disease progressed, reading about fits and fainting.

Meanwhile, Danilo was becoming more and more confident that he would win the election, and all the polls said he was firmly in first place with the PRM party man in second, and the current mayor a long way behind in third. He was working every hour and called me every couple of days to check all was well and to ask me to raise more money – not necessarily in that order.

Belinda had been on the diuretics for three days and was fine. It was around four in the afternoon and I was busy at the computer watching her as she was playing with the puppies and the three of them were bounding over the sofa and the chairs. Suddenly, she let out a high-pitched scream, the like of which I had never heard from a dog, and she fell over. The puppies looked puzzled and backed away as I ran over to her, assuming she had fainted. She hadn't fainted, she was dead.

"Oh my God, Belinda," I said to her, and frantically tried to do CPR but to no avail. What on earth was I to do with a hundred and thirty pound dead Great Dane lying in the middle of my living room? Firstly I ran upstairs to get a signal on the phone and called Angela.

"Angela, Belinda is dead and I need help to bury her," I panted down the phone, breathless and shaking.

"Lindsay, I am not in Cacique. Go to my house and ask Leopoldo to come and help you," she answered. I hesitated, not really sure what to do, so I called Danilo although I don't know what I expected him to do.

"Danilo, Belinda is dead. She is lying in the middle of the living room floor."

"Call Angela," he instructed. "She can help round up neighbours to help bury her."

"I have, you idiot, but she isn't here," I answered crossly.

"Well, go and find someone else," he said. "I am in a meeting."

"There is no one else," I screamed down the phone. "All the neighbours are dead or bloody useless. You have to help me," I yelled. "I can't do this! I cannot do this anymore. You have to help, you have to!" But I was screaming to a dead phone.

I wandered downstairs, hoping I had made a mistake, but Belinda was still dead. I locked up the other dogs so that if I did find someone they would not be scared to come in the house, and I set off to find the neighbours. First port of call was Miguel, who was at the back of his house sitting at the little wooden table.

"Miguel, the big dog is dead, can you help me bury her?" I asked.

"The big dog? No, she will weigh too much for my heart," he answered, walking to his motorbike and throwing his leg over it before setting off at speed down the road.

"Ask Berto," he yelled as he drove off.

"Yeah, right, "I muttered under my breath. "Berto who is too scared of everything, I can't see him helping as he never has before." I wandered out of the front of Miguel's house just in time to see Leopoldo riding his motorbike off in the other direction, as a toothless, craggy faced man called Tany, who lived further up the road, was walking towards me. He was also called *Mano Tibia*, which means warm hand – no idea why.

"Thank goodness. Tany can you help me bury Belinda, the big dog, she has died and is lying in the living room," I asked him hurriedly.

He took a big draw on his *Nacional* cigarette and said, "Sure, but we will need help as she is a massive dog, let's ask Berto, I know he is there as I have just seen him."

We walked into Berto's garden and Tany yelled out.

"Berto, we need your help to bury a dog,"

Berto appeared from inside the garage.

"Oh, I don't think I can help much," he said, unsurprisingly.

"Of course you can," said Tany brusquely. "It will only take a minute, now come on, hurry up as I need to get to the church." And with that he almost physically dragged Berto round to the house.

"The other dogs are locked up so don't worry," I explained. "And I have the wheelbarrow here so you can just wheel her to the pet graveyard, which is in the hollow in the back garden."

We needed to get Belinda down ten concrete steps from the living room into the back garden and then wheel her to the animal cemetery about eight hundred metres away.

Tany looked at the wheelbarrow.

"Well, that won't work, it's punctured," he observed, and then he and Berto came into the house and stood there looking down at Belinda lying where she had fallen on the white tiled floor next to the sofa in the middle of the living room.

"Well, we can't touch her," he said.

"Why not?" I asked.

"Because you can't touch dead dogs," he replied. "To be honest you shouldn't even touch dogs when they are alive either," he continued.

"I have some thick plastic bags which had dog food in. Do you want me to wrap her in those somehow?"

"Don't worry," said Tany, and he beckoned Berto and the two of them disappeared into the back garden and started pulling down fronds from the palm trees and plaiting them.

They returned with the plaited palm leaves, which now looked like a green-knotted rope and slipped the noose of it over Belinda's head, without touching her. Then, leaving me standing there aghast they dragged all one hundred and thirty pounds of her, through the living room and down the ten concrete steps into the garden, her inert body smashing down on each step and then they simply dragged her like a sack of coal through the back garden and the undergrowth until they were lost from view.

I stood numb with the awfulness of it, shoulders slumped and heart pounding, until they returned.

"Thank you, thank you, sooo much," I said, as they arrived back at the back of the house. "She is buried, yes?"

"No, she is down there, we don't have time to bury her," replied Tany. "You will have to do that." And with that, they left.

I couldn't do it. I couldn't face walking down the garden and seeing her lying there. I couldn't face digging a grave and pushing her into it. I just could not do it. But with a heavy heart I knew I would have to, but I really had no idea how, so I just slumped down onto the sofa with my head in my hands, hoping for a miracle and for me to find the strength from somewhere to do what had to be done.

The miracle appeared in the guise of stepsons Dany and Alberto. Danilo had called them and instructed them to come and help and they had sped over on a motorbike. They ran into the house.

"Where is she?" demanded Dany. "We don't have much time as it is getting dark and it is dangerous driving back from here in the dark."

"Out there. In the pet graveyard. They dragged her there and left her, but she needs burying. I don't know exactly where they left her."

Dany and Alberto gathered up a pickaxe and a shovel and marched off down the garden. They returned around half an hour later. Alberto looked sick.

"That was horrible," he announced.

"Have you done it, is she properly buried?" I asked.

"Yes, it's done," replied Dany.

"Thanks boys so much, you saved my life as no way could I do that," I said gratefully, giving them a hug before they jumped back on the motorbike and left, leaving me alone yet again.

Belinda was a fabulous dog and well loved and over the next few days I thanked her for not putting me through days, weeks or even months of watching her deteriorate as her heart became worse. The house was deadly quiet without her, even the dogs were silent, and every evening as I sat down to watch television I missed her presence lying next to me on the sofa with her head in my lap, which was our ritual every night.

I was often one to say, *"I don't know what I will do if anything happens to xyz cat or dog,"* but now I know. It is very sad, but I have learned I can cope alone if a dog has a heart attack and dies in front of me, it will not always be in an antiseptic vet's office and you will not always have anyone with you. I can cope if I am alone and have to deal with the situation. You think *"I can't,"* then you realise, *"I can,"* and then you can say *"and I did"*.

Bit by bit I could feel myself becoming more Dominican. Having to deal with so many deaths of people and pets, each one hardened me more. Of course I was sad, of course I missed them, but I learned that the only person in charge of your emotions is you, no one else. You can allow yourself to be sad and feel pain, but not for long, as if you wallow in it the only person you hurt most is yourself.

We had visitors all of the time at Wasp House. Most only stayed for a day or two, but every couple of months the house had to be cleaned ready for the latest arrival. Not that we didn't clean in between times, but it had a special clean when visitors were coming.

Many of the visitors I had never physically met, but met online via DR Sisterhood. Some came alone, some with their boyfriends, fiancés and husbands. Some came so I could check out their other halves and advise them whether or not they were sanky pankies. In addition, some expats came to stay, especially those who lived in towns or cities where it was hot in the summer, and here it was much cooler and quieter. Shirley came for Christmas one year, Ro came and we had a fabulous time, and Grace and Nany came too.

Some of the visitors loved it here, they loved the countryside, the dogs and the chickens, and revelled in the 'glamping' style of life we had with open windows all of the time. Others found it hard going.

"Where's the air conditioning?"

"Where are the mosquito screens for the windows?"

"There aren't any," I would reply, making a mental note to buy a mosquito net for the guest bed.

"Why can't I drink the water out of the tap?"

"Well, you can if you want cholera or dysentery," I would reply.

When visitors arrived for the first time I would take them around the house with a list of instructions. I must admit it seemed like there were a lot, but I had just got used to them.

"This is the bathroom. Please do not put your toilet paper in the toilet as there is no mains sewage and it doesn't bounce like poo does so will clog up the pipes and block the toilet. Just put it in this bin here." The usual reply to this was, "Ewwww!"

I would explain about not drinking the water, keeping the gate to the kitchen closed so the puppies would not go in the kitchen bin, turning the hot water on twenty minutes before they wanted a shower and remembering to turn it off. If we were low on water – the water only came once every two weeks to fill the cistern – I would ask them not to use too much.

Food was a major issue. Many did not eat certain things such as rice, salad, onions, fish, spicy food, which make it a bit of a challenge to cook. Others had not seen what I call real food.

"What are you doing Lindsay?"

"Cutting up potatoes for chips."

"French fries come from potatoes?"

Others came across things they had never eaten before such as Dominican root vegetables, plantains and even avocados. Some had never seen some foodstuffs in their natural form.

"What's this stick-like thing?"

"Ginger," I would reply.

"Oh my God, I thought it just came in powder," would be the reply.

"And this funny white thing?"

"Garlic."

"You don't buy it in jars, in paste?"

"Nope."

"Why has this egg got brown stuff on it?"

"That's chicken shit, they often shit when giving birth to an egg."

Most were appalled at the way we bought meat, seeing the pig butcher cutting up an actual pig, or buying chickens with their neck and feet on. One lady had no idea chickens had bones as she always bought her chicken boneless, and she would watch me with morbid fascination as I cut a raw chicken up.

Many visitors had no idea you could make pastry without buying it in a packet, you could make apple pie with apples and not a tin of apple pie mix, you could make cakes with flour, butter, eggs, milk and sugar and not a packet mix; that soup was made with water and vegetables and did not come in a tin. I really began to think I was living on a different planet.

Despite all the hard work when visitors came, cleaning and cooking, it was always lovely to speak English and they all would bring me goodies such as dog toys, chocolate and especially things I missed from England like walnut whips, Bisto and Oxo cubes, Bird's Custard and Cadbury's drinking chocolate.

Many of the couples, English speaking women from Canada, or the US or the UK usually along with a Dominican man, could not speak each other's language so I would translate. If I wasn't around they communicated via their smartphones using Google translate or another online translation programme. Lynne was by now seeing the guy she had met in Barahona – Eneef, as Danilo called him – and they came to stay and eventually she took him to the US on a fiancé visa and they married, so that was a happy ending. Others came with men who were obvious sankies, some brought men they assumed were Dominicans, but they were actually Haitian and the women could not tell. Not that it mattered, apart from when it came to getting a visa, especially if their identity card was false and many Haitians living in the Dominican Republic had fake ID cards. There was pretty much a constant stream of visitors every couple of months, which kept the house clean and me in chocolate.

There were some changes happening with the elections, which should have been for the good. In the municipality of Guayacanes they had what they called *mesas* or tables, each one having a certain number of people voting there. There was one table in each of the smaller communities and up to four in the larger areas with a larger population. Previously, people voted, folded up their ballot papers and stuffed them into the ballot box. At the end of the day the votes would be counted.

This year, for the first time, it was supposed to be electronic counting in that the ballots would be scanned and put through a machine, which took the count directly to the Central Electoral Court (JCE). I thought this would mean less chance for fraud – a great thing.

The day of the election came closer and closer and I began to allow myself to imagine what would happen when he won. I had said as soon as I knew he had won I would go down there, but not before. I sorted out the clothes I would wear and my daily feeling of stress began to be replaced by excited nervousness.

The day arrived and I was on tenterhooks waiting for the result. Danilo called me at around 9pm.

"Hola Primera Dama. Hi First Lady. I have won."

"What? How do you know? It is too early."

"I has delegate in each voting centre to make sure all okay. Delegates they say I win. I many win. No one close. I win every *mesa*."

As the votes were submitted to the JCE (the Central Electoral Court) they issued bulletins. In the first bulletin, with over 11% of votes counted, Danilo was in the lead with 33.23% of the votes. Second was Noel with 23.42% (he was with the PRM) and third the current mayor with 22.47%. Danilo was around ten percentage points in the lead. Now I know statistics and that was unlikely to change much. The relief was overwhelming and I went to sleep easily, with a smile on my face, looking forward to the morning and the congratulatory phone calls which would come.

It was not to be. Everything went horribly wrong. As the votes for each centre were counted they should have been scanned using the new machines. But the majority of the voting centres in Guayacanes had no electricity, most had no Internet, some had no idea how to use the machine and some didn't know the password, so in the end the counting was done manually and the law said that the manual count would override the electronic count. Total waste of millions of pesos.

The results for each *mesa* were entered onto what is called an *Acta*. These were taken to the main office in Guayacanes for sending on to the JCE. All of the delegates went to the main office in Guayacanes with the ballot papers and the *Actas,* and the Head of the local Electoral Court submitted the first bulletin. He could see from the other *Actas* that Danilo had won by miles. He told the staff it had been a long day and to go home and they would finish off in the morning. The people in the local Electoral court should be supervised by the candidates or their delegates to see again no funny business. But when the office was closed, in the middle of the night, the members of the local electoral court went in with members of the existing local government and changed the numbers on the *Actas.* When the delegates and candidates returned in the morning the *Actas* had been changed, new bulletins issued and votes had been taken off Danilo and given to the existing mayor. By the following morning the existing mayor was in the lead with 31% of the votes and Danilo had crashed down to 22%.

Impossible. He complained along with the other candidates, they went on television, they went to court and the case was ruled inadmissible. The JCE then forbade any recounts or any rechecking of the *Actas*.

This happened in another twenty-nine municipalities throughout the country. People were complaining, burning local election offices. Their votes were worth nothing. You all know I love this country, but here there is no democracy.

Guayacanes had the chance to have a mayor who would do all he could to improve the lives of the people there, and they voted for him. But due to the local head of the electoral court, and the massive corrupt nature of the current mayor, their votes were worth nothing. There is no point in having elections here, just a huge waste of time and money. There is no point in having an electoral judiciary, as the Dominicans are incapable of delivering justice. We hoped something would happen and, as before, we spent money we did not have going to court and fighting, and this time there were protests, complaints, hunger strikes and riots across the country. And the new government said not a word. Danilo Medina had an overwhelming victory, but did not comment at all on what happened. It just went away.

I called Danilo on the Wednesday after the elections on the Sunday.

"Come home. *Ya* it's over. You can't fight it so let's get back to where we were, you study to be a lawyer, I will keep working. This time we still have the house. Please just come home."

And he did, and we returned to normal life once again. Thank goodness, the relief was simply overwhelming. My dad once said to me, "Don't find a man you can live with, find one you can't live without." I now realised I could not live without Danilo.

CHAPTER NINE
ALBERT

"Avoid loud and aggressive persons,
they are vexations to the spirit."
Desiderata, Max Ehrmann 1927

CAST YOUR MINDS BACK TO JUAN DOLIO ON THE SOUTH COAST OF the country where we used to live. Danilo had one full brother and two full sisters, but his mother had had more children before she ended up with Danilo's father, and more after she left him. Each child had a different father and Danilo really had no idea how many there were. One of them was Antonio, who was about ten years older than Danilo. As soon as Danilo and I were living together, so in the early 2000s, he started turning up at our house from San Francisco de Macoris in the centre of the country where he was living. He would just call to visit, eat, drink my rum and then disappear. I didn't realize at the time that he had moved to Juan Dolio and was living in a cheap guest house, enjoying the pleasures which life had to offer, including Yolanda, a very tall, very beautiful Haitian prostitute.

Eventually he moved into a house with Chi Chi (remember him from *What About Your Saucepans?* He was the guy who had sex with a donkey) and we would see him from time to time, Danilo more than me.

Anyway, one day Antonio opened the little door in the middle of the gate in our villa in Juan Dolio, shoved this little fat black toddler through the gate, closed it and disappeared. The child ran screaming down the garden watched by the dogs.

"Danilo!" I screamed. "What has your brother just pushed through the gate?"

Danilo came out and laughed, "That is Chocolatay," he said, walking quickly through the garden to pick up the dirty, snotty nosed child, who would not stop screaming.

"Who the hell is Chocolatay?" I asked.

"Antonio's son," he replied. "He didn't pay child support, so mother gives child to him. You know here that men have boy children and women have girl childrens. Antonio has him as he no pay."

"And who is the mother? And where is the mother now?" I demanded.

"Mother is Yolanda," he replied.

"The Haitian hooker?"

"*Si.* She say Antonio is father."

I did not warm to Chocolate. Antonio would shove him in the gate every so often – the child would not speak, just scream and hated the dogs. And to be honest I didn't think much about him and when we left Juan Dolio I never thought of him again.

Fast forward again to 2013 when we were living in Wasp House and Chivirico came for lunch with Dany, Alberto and Ana, along with a lanky child who was almost as tall as me. He was thin, sullen, did not appear to have much personality and didn't say a word. When they arrived Danilo grabbed hold of him and pulled him towards me, laughing.

"Lindsay look, this is Chocolatay," he yelled.

"Who?" I said, racking my brain as I was wiping my hands on the tea towel.

"Antonio son. Albert."

"Oh, hi Albert," I said, stretching out my hand, which the child took limply and disinterestedly. "What's he doing here," I hissed under my breath, dragging Danilo back to the kitchen.

"He live in Esperanza now," hissed Danilo back at me. "I *splain* later."

And splain he did as only Danilo can, on a need to know basis.

What he told me was that on one of his trips back down south, Dany had found Albert on the beach in Juan Dolio, semi-naked and begging. He was starving and although he was aged eight, was not going to school. I am not sure if he was living with his mother or father or nobody, I did know that Antonio was not working as he had had a stroke, and would have been in his late fifties by then. So apparently, Albert being family, Dany had brought him to Esperanza and he initially lived with a lady there who lived alone. Many people like having a child in the house to do chores and for company. He was going to school as well. It appears that for some reason the lady did not want him to live there anymore, though I have no idea why, being told things on a need to know basis, so when Ana and Alberto got together, he moved in with them. In one bedroom there was Ana, Alberto and the baby, and in the other Dany, and Albert and Christian when he came back from Spain.

That was all the information I had and every so often, over the next year or so, Albert would turn up with the boys a few times a year, never spoke much, never smiled.

In August 2016 Danilo had left to run errands and visit the boys in Esperanza, and when he came home Albert was with him. With a suitcase. I just stared as he walked through the door with a sick, sinking feeling in my stomach.

"De Fe!" yelled Danilo in greeting. I did not reply, but just stared at him.

"Albert come to live with us now," he shouted, and then quickly took Albert upstairs to what I called Chivirico's bedroom. When Danilo came back downstairs again, somewhat sheepishly, I dragged him by the arm into the kitchen.

"Now you can bloody well splain. And it doesn't matter what you say the answer is N.O. No, no way, not now, not ever, never, NO. You cannot just bring a child to live here without discussing it with me. That is not how it works. You should have asked me first."

"You say 'no' if I ask you, so I no ask you," he said grinning.

"Well, I say no now. One night, he leaves tomorrow. I do not want another child in this house. I went through it with Dany and Alberto, and I am not doing it again."

"But you like Chivirico, you want him to stay here, why not Albert?" he argued

"Chiv is Chiv. I like him. I do not like Albert. I have no emotional bond with him."

"But Albert, he has nowhere to go. Alberto he has no job as his company gone now. Dany, he has no job. Ana has no job. They have no money for food and no money for Albert. I know what it is like to be poor and has nothing. Albert has nothing, no one, he has to have chance. I say he stay here. He no trouble, he go to school, he help you in house."

Faced with blatant emotional blackmail, Albert stayed.

It was obvious very quickly that Albert had issues, and I had no idea how to deal with them. He forgot everything. He forgot to close the fridge door and forgot to close the gate into the kitchen. Danilo and I went out to pay our respects to Angela, the *bruja*, when her mother died, just for an hour and when we returned the gate to the kitchen was open and the fridge door was open and the dogs had taken everything out of the fridge and had a feast. The place was a total mess. He forgot to close the front door, he forgot to close the big gate into the garden so the dogs all escaped, not once but three times. He never flushed the toilet, used a roll of toilet paper a day, and we had no idea why. He forgot to wear shoes, always going barefoot inside and out. He forgot to get changed for bed and slept in his clothes. He forgot to turn the hot water off, turn lights off.

All he wanted to do was watch television, cartoons. His table manners were off the charts. He preferred to eat with his hands, and was always sick with stomach problems as his hands were filthy and he forgot to wash them. He would eat the bones from chickens, take food from the fridge all the time and store it in his bedroom. The bedroom was not just messy as kids' bedrooms are: it was disgusting with rotting food and dirty plates under the bed and shoved into drawers.

He was arrogant, which I had never seen in a Dominican child before. He would answer back and always knew best. There was no question he was bright, very, very bright, especially at maths, but he was cocky with it. We enrolled him in the local school, and for that needed his birth certificate, which had Yolanda as his mother, but no father. So who the hell was his father? And if it wasn't Antonio why was he here?

I asked Danilo.

"Look there is no father on the birth certificate, so who is his father?"

"She say Antonio, but he no know. Albert look like Johnny, *motoconcho* driver. He is boyfren of Yolanda. She has four or fy chilrens with him and Albert look like them too."

Albert wasn't all bad. He would go to the *colmado*, sweep and mop the floors, do the dishes at night, do his own washing and get himself to school. But he started to be sneaky and lying and stealing. The lies were so obvious in that he would say he had won at baseball, but the manager would tell Danilo they had lost. When asked why he lied, he would just say *"por na"* and shrug his shoulders. That means, 'for no reason'.

We were called into the school every few weeks about his behaviour. Running down the stairs, being rude to the teachers, even cutting a fellow pupil's backpack with scissors. All was *'por na'*. I was talking to Ana about it and she said when he was living with them she was called in daily, so she thought he must be improving. Funny no one mentioned his behaviour to me when I was told he was going to live here.

We enrolled him in baseball classes and as he was so tall for his age there was a tiny possibility he might be good at baseball, and he certainly enjoyed it and took it seriously going to all the games and the practice sessions.

I checked online to see if I could get any help on how to deal with his behaviour and how to get it to change and all I found out was that he probably was suffering from a whole series of letters such as ADS, ODD, ADHD and whatever else. Most of the recommendations involved taking the child to a psychiatrist, which wasn't going to happen as there were none within reasonable distance.

Slowly he began to improve. I encouraged him to cook, as I had Chivirico, and having made pizza from scratch only once he could do it again and again. How could he remember a complicated recipe for dough and tomato sauce and not remember to flush the toilet? He would always cook his own tea after school and only set fire to the stove twice. We were slowly taking two steps forward and one back and even the school called to say his behaviour was much improved.

Chivirico would come for the weekends still and the two had a good relationship. Albert used to have problems with playing well and in a friendly manner, screaming '*mentira*' (meaning 'liar') all the time, and cheating, but bit by bit that lessened, although it didn't totally stop.

I would try and talk to him when I could, and slowly he began to open up.

"So, what is your first memory?" I asked, as we were peeling potatoes together.

"Living with my mother in Los Conocos, and going to pre-school," he replied. "Then I went to live with my father when he lived opposite your house, which is when I met you and Tio Danilo."

"Can you remember me and uncle Danilo?" I asked.

"Yes, a bit, and I remember the dogs as I was terrified of them," he said laughing. "Then my mum came with the police and took me away as my dad didn't want to give me back. But they took me away and my grandmother took me to Haiti."

"So, can you speak Creole? And what is Haiti like?" I questioned, being interested, as I had never been to Haiti.

"Not any more, I have forgotten. Haiti is hot. Very hot and

very dusty. There are no trees, just a lot of dust," he said. "I wanted to come home, so after two years I came back and lived with my mum in the house you and Danilo and Dany and Alberto lived in."

"Which house was that?"

"The one opposite Guavaberry Beach Club."

"Oh yes, with the gay Italian living upstairs, Oscar," I remembered.

"We didn't live in the main house, we lived in the little room at the bottom of the garden," Albert said.

"Oh the one Chi Chi used to live in? The watchyman house?"

"Yes, that's it."

"So what happened then?" I asked.

"Well, I lived there with my mum, but she often went away so I was on my own," he reminisced.

"Where did she go to? And how long for?" I asked.

"I don't know. She never told me. She just wasn't there sometimes. For one week, maybe two."

"So who looked after you?"

"No one. I looked after myself. I was like seven to nine years old. I was very hungry, sometimes didn't eat for many days, so I would go onto the beach and ask people for money."

"Did you get much money?" I asked, fascinated.

"Not much. And then Dany saw me one day and then my father put me on a bus to Santiago and Dany was there in Santiago and took me to Esperanza. And that is it."

Was it the Jesuits who said, "Give me a child till he is seven and I will show you the man?" Would that first seven years rule his behaviour for the rest of his life or could we turn it round? Only time would tell.

Wasp house was an odd house as upstairs the interior walls did not reach the roof – there was a gap of three feet and there was a gap of around one foot around the outside which allowed the hot air to escape and the bats to fly in. The roof was the interesting part being made of wood with asphalt material on top of it, and sort of balanced on a piece of wood in each corner and then had the gap between the roof and the wall.

Most Dominican houses are built like this as it allows the hot air to escape and keeps the house cool. Mind you, most have zinc roofs and not plywood. The roof was actually very attractive from underneath – very rustic, apart from the edge bits where it was sort of coming apart and had a few holes in it where the Internet man walked on it in hobnail boots to fix the thirty-foot aerial on the roof.

Anyway, me being British, I thought people should have a bit of privacy in the bedroom and bathroom so when Danilo was designing and finishing off the house, before we moved in, I asked him to make the walls on the inside go up to the roof and the ones on the outside still leave a little gap for the hot air to escape. Apart from between our bedroom and the guest room – which means that noises, any noises, from one bedroom travel to the other. It wasn't boarded between the two rooms as we originally had been waiting for wardrobes to be fitted, which they now have been for over three years.

I went to bed as usual before Danilo, and Albert was already in bed. That was one thing he did well, in that he knew bed time was 10pm at the latest so would always be sound asleep by then – like all Dominicans I knew, sleep was something he could do anytime and anywhere.

Danilo was downstairs studying and watching television, as

when I go to bed I go to sleep and if there is someone next to me watching television at Dominican volume and commenting on the programme – usually the History Channel or National Geographic – and asking me questions all the time, jabbing me with his elbow if I don't answer, I get grouchy. Extremely grouchy. So the law is when I go to bed, if he wanted to keep watching television, he went downstairs to watch it.

I was lying in bed in the dark, writing chapter five of this book in my head, and listening to the noise outside, so I could describe nights in the *campo*. The crickets squeaking, the limpkins squawking and the occasional noise from the roof. We have always wondered what the noise on the roof was – apparently the naked backward-feet woman, remember? – as nothing can get onto the roof from the house, so I assumed it was a chicken or a bird.

Then there was a noise of something falling in the bedroom. I assumed it was the cat or the puppy, but they didn't answer when I called, so I got out of bed and turned on the light and there it was. A rat. It was on top of our wardrobe, between us and the guest room, and ran around on top of the wall and looked at me.

Now, Dominican rats are not like British rats. I had lived in houses in London where rats in the garden were commonplace and I think they say that in London you are never more than ten feet – or is it yards? – from a rat. British rats are big with thick tails. They also have very, very big teeth and are really appalling. Think bubonic plague. Think around twelve-inches long and evil looking buggers.

However, Dominican rats are actually cute as rats go. Long whiskers, much smaller, not as dark and halfway between the size of a British mouse and a British rat. I ran downstairs and said to Danilo,

"Rat in the bedroom. It's on top of the wardrobe."

Danilo wandered upstairs, but there was no sign of the rat, not surprising as it had the whole upstairs to explore, plus balconies, and could run around on the tops of all of the walls and, if needed to, duck inside the gaps in the concrete blocks which the walls were made of. But unless rats jump thirty feet to the ground (do they?) it couldn't get out.

Danilo was his usual blasé self.

"All houses have rats. It is no problem. A rat is a rat."

"Well, call me a wuss, but I really don't want a rat in my bedroom and where there is one rat there will be more. I think they must be a new arrival as I've never seen them before and the cats catch everything that moves, but they have never brought in a rat. I'm deducing it could be linked to Albert's arrival and his habit of eating all day long, either in his bedroom or watching the television, and having zero concept of not throwing food or wrappers or fruit peelings on the floor or under the bed. You will get rid of the rat. No question. Just do it. I do not do rats."

The trouble was we had visitors arriving in twelve days who would be staying in the guest room, and I am not sure people from overseas would be quite as chilled at the idea of having a rat watching them from the top of the wardrobe. Especially as the people coming – Lynne and Eneef – had not seen each other for months. I could just see a whole gathering of rats on top of the wardrobe gawking at the activity in the guest room.

So, I had to solve the problem. Solution one was to get rid of rats. Now being a kind soul I didn't necessarily want to kill them and wouldn't use poison with dogs, cats and people in the house. I couldn't stand the noise that rattraps made, nor the mess, so I went to the village shop and bought the famous Dominican product, The End to the Rat, or even The Rat Meets a Sticky End. This was a sticky pad, but while the rat would stick to it, you couldn't unstick it and the man in the shop explained

I would then have to kill it with a machete. I sent Danilo to buy a rattrap.

The rattrap was set using Canadian cheddar as Danilo didn't think rats would like Dominican cheese – nor did I. It was caught in the Christmas tree on top of Albert's wardrobe. A week later the television in our bedroom had a picture which was red, and on opening the back there was a baby rat asleep inside and all the wires chewed. Baby rat two ate my recipes and was caught in the cupboard inside a box of tea bags. Baby rat three was caught in the study and baby rat four was thought to be the one that ate the thermostat in the back of the fridge.

Christmas approached once again and, had it not been for the kids, Albert and Chivirico, we would probably have treated it as just another day, but they were desperate to write their lists for Santa Claus and put up the tree – so both were done. The tree appeared to have lost many of its baubles, but was fine and amazingly the lights still worked. The fairy had no head as Pandora had eaten it, so was replaced by a little bear.

The lists for Santa were identical for both and not quite the same as the lists Santa had from Dany and Alberto some fifteen years or so previously, which were – one T-shirt, one pair of tennis shoes, one pencil and Albert wanted peanut butter. These lists were long, brand orientated and expensive – iPad (Aipa), iPhone, tablet, laptop, Jordan and Nike tennis shoes, five T-shirts, five pairs of trousers, radio controlled car, plane, helicopter, loads of baseball gear, roller skates, bicycle and buoquitoki (walkie talkie) etc. etc. Santa nearly had a heart attack. Luckily, I had been busy with work doing lots of translations in November so we could just manage one thing each – a tablet – made in China.

Albert went to Esperanza to stay with Chivirico for the

few days before Christmas giving Danilo a chance to wrap presents. Danilo adored Christmas and had done all of the shopping, including for himself, so I had no idea what I was supposedly giving him. It turned out to be a sweatshirt and he had toothpaste from the dogs and soap from the cats. He bought me two pairs of knickers – one with a wifi symbol on the front and another with a start button. I think they would go down a treat in Marks and Spencer. Given that Dany, Alberto and Ana were out of work, he bought presents for everyone to give everyone – I even had a pack of cotton buds from Saya to clean my laptop with.

I was going to cook British Christmas turkey lunch as I always did, so I needed to know what time I should cook for and for how many.

"How many people are coming for British Christmas lunch, Danilo?" I asked him the day before.

"I no know, between six and (counts on fingers) fifteen maybe. Or maybe more," he replied.

"What time are they arriving Danilo?"

"I no know. Between maybe 10am and 7pm."

This took flexibility and patience to a whole new level so I decided to do a Dominican/ British fusion lunch, which would not spoil if it sat there for hours. So we had turkey, but rice and peas instead of roast potatoes, and Russian salad, instead of sprouts, and parsnips and cranberry sauce and stuffing and Christmas pudding.

On Christmas day, the kids arrived along with Alberto and Dany, Ana and grandbaby and Saya the dwendy and some strange man. We always seem to have strange men here for Christmas lunch, but at least it was only one strange man so there would be plenty of food. Having opened the presents the kids found a note in the bottom of their stockings (which were full of things like deodorant, soap, an apple, socks), sending them off on a treasure hunt to find Santa's gifts, which caused great excitement and pure joy when they discovered their tablets.

Just before lunch the boys all went out to check on Danilo's latest money making venture – honey making. He had a little swarm of bees living in a cat carrier (no idea how) and had built a beehive out of the wardrobe door.

Beeman had been previously and transferred the bees, including the Queen, to the new beehive so the menfolk went to check on the bees, while yours truly cooked lunch. Disaster, the bees had gone on holiday. Beeman was called (yes, it was Christmas day) and collected in our car, along with his six kids. He announced the queen had left and there were no more bees. End of money-making project. Danilo invited him and his kids for lunch (while I silently panicked), but when Danilo said it was English food, they made their apologies and left.

Chivirico stayed for the whole of the holidays and the three kids – Albert, Chiv and Danilo (the big kid), played together all day long. Danilo asked if they wanted to play *pico gallo* ('pico' means a beak and 'gallo' is a cockerel or rooster). They excitedly said yes and rushed outside to see how to play. Danilo demonstrated putting a six-inch long bread roll in his crotch with a bit sticking out and letting the roosters fly up and peck it. Peck the pecker. I was laughing too much to take photos and the kids refused to play, even for a hundred pesos. But the money went up and eventually Danilo offered a thousand pesos to the winner – the one whose bread was pecked off first. The temptation was too great, but they decided to go one more, and I was distractedly working on the computer when I looked up to see Albert and Chivirico taping a bread roll each to their willies with black electrical tape. They asked me to go outside and video them playing *pico gallo*. I explained I did not want to be arrested for child abuse, so persuaded them to unstick the bread rolls (harder than sticking them on) and just put the bread in their hands.

Every day was a new challenge for the boys, ranging from building more chicken houses, to building the wall, to cooking cup cakes, birthday cakes, playing chess, planting avocados, making pancakes and when the end of the holidays came, I was grateful for the return to normality although I missed the constant laughter.

CHAPTER TEN
CHOICES

*"You are a child of the universe, no less than the
trees and the stars; you have a right to be here."*
Desiderata, Max Ehrmann 1927

THE PROBLEMS WITH THE NEIGHBOURS AT THE FRONT CONTINUED.
They had fewer chickens now, and the male dogs were locked
up in the doghouse in the day, but allowed out in the front
garden in the afternoon. Meg, Grita and the puppy, Canguro,
were kept in the house as the first two were in heat, although
I would let Canguro out with the males for an hour or so. She
was very cute, daughter of Lobo and Grita, who Danilo had let
out on her previous heat and was around four months old.

One day, Danilo was at university and a chicken flew over from the neighbours into our garden and the dogs chased it, but fortunately the chicken managed to fly away. Feluche, the old man, was standing near the fighting cocks waving his machete at me.

"I am going to kill those bloody dogs," he screamed manically, waving his machete above his head.

I ignored him, locked the dogs back in the doghouse and walked back inside.

A few days later, Rin Tin Tin stopped eating and wasn't happy so I let him spend the night outside on his own, thinking the male dogs were bullying him with the females on heat. In the morning he still didn't want to eat and I could tell something was wrong with him. I gave him water and he drank loads, but then he vomited and his back legs went. Within minutes he lay down, looking at me so soulfully with his big brown eyes, suddenly pints of blood poured out of his rear end, his tongue flopped out of his mouth and he was dead.

"Danilo," I screamed, and Danilo came running downstairs.

"This is rat poison," he said grimly, and went on to tell me that Berto had told him they had put poison down as they had so many rats. It wasn't surprising as they had cows and a horse as well as all the chickens, with stacks of hay for the cows. All I could do was to pray that the others would be all right.

The treatment for rat poison in dogs is vitamin K, which has to be given as soon as possible after the poisoning. Rat poison causes the animals to bleed to death internally, but vitamin K helps to clot the blood. Just in case the others had also been poisoned I rushed to Monción to try and get some vitamin K, but there was none to be found.

That night Sweepy was sick. The next morning Grita and Canguru were both sick and had diarrhoea. Over the next few days Danilo and I spent all of our time cleaning up diarrhoea and vomit. Danilo went to the *agroveterinaria* and came back with injections for all of them – anti virals, antibiotics, and rehydration fluid and we started on the fight to try and save them and not for the first time I wished there was a decent vet here as I filled up syringes and injected the dogs.

Grita was the next to die. She was just lying at my feet as she always did when suddenly, just like Rin Tin Tin, pints of blood poured out of her and she was gone. Next was Sweepy. Each time, Danilo would put them in the wheelbarrow and wheel them down to the now full pet cemetery.

Meg and Lobo were the only two not to be affected. In the meantime I was just hoping we could save Canguru the puppy, but things were not looking good. To be honest I thought she would be the first to go being the smallest, but she was still vomiting and still not eating and was more or less unconscious.

Another day went past and I was working at the computer as usual with Canguru lying next to me on the floor. Danilo was cooking in the kitchen, when Canguru stood up and started to move. *Here we go,* I thought, *steel yourself to clean up more vomit or diarrhoea*. But no. She walked unsteadily into the kitchen, sat down next to Danilo asking for food.

"De Fe!" he shouted. "She wants food! She will be fine now. No die."

And she got better and better. But we were left with just Lobo, faithful old Meg and Canguru and we both knew that something had to be done. We had no proof it was rat poison, although it looked like it, but we knew that if a rat had been poisoned and then the dogs ate it then they would suffer as well. Just we did not think they would eat a rat. We knew the neighbours, well some of them, did not like the dogs and we knew they used poison although they subsequently denied it.

And we hated the fighting cockerels right next to the fence. So we decided to build the Great Wall of Cacique.

Luckily, I had quite a lot of work so we could afford to at least start and within no time at all the concrete blocks were delivered and the sand, gravel, metal bars and cement. Danilo said that he and Saya would do it to save on labour and sometimes Dany and Alberto came to help.

Part one was to take down the wooden stick fence and dig footings, fill them with concrete and metal bars. Then Saya laid the blocks and he even used a spirit level, which was amazing. Within no time at all we had the wall between us and the neighbours finished and then started on the sides. When we ran out of money we stopped, but each time we had the odd hundred pounds or two hundred dollars we bought more blocks. Everything came to a standstill once Danilo went back to university as he was taking six subjects, which would mean if he passed them all he would only have one semester left to do until he was a fully qualified lawyer. We were waiting for his next break to get on with more of it, and his latest plan was to build the wall all around the front of the house and then down into the back garden and across the back garden.

"Danilo, that is a lot of wall and a lot of money," I warned.

"Yes bow dogs have more spay then. They can go every places front and back," he replied in explanation.

"Yes bow... sorry but, the dogs will chase your chickens which are in the back garden," I pointed out.

"No becow my chicking go other side of wall in other feel," he said confidently.

"They will fly over the bloody wall," I retorted.

"No, becow chicking no fly over walls," he said knowledgably. "And with chicking we have goat and sheeps."

"We do? What is this? Money making venture number ninety-three?"

"We may many money from goat and sheeps and I tee you how get milk from them," he laughed.

So once the wall is finished, we are going into the sheep and goat business, apparently.

Danilo continued to build things around the house, and I never had any idea what he was up to until things disappeared.

Me: "Danilo where is the chopping board?"

Danilo: "Shopping bow?"

Me: "Chopping board numpty. To chop things like vegetables."

Danilo: "Numpty?"

Me: "Don't change the subject. Where is it? I have three – small, medium, large. The large one has gone."

Danilo: "The one that is sort of the right size for a door to a new chicking how?"

Me: "Oh shit."

Everything was back to normal after the second political shenanigans. I am still writing and working, Danilo is back at university, the only difference from when we arrived in Wasp House is that we have fewer dogs, fewer cats, more chickens and Albert. I am now sixty-one years old – a horrid thought and it is time for reflection.

Almost all of the reviews for *What about your Saucepans?* were four or five star, which is very gratifying. However, there was one two star, and the person who wrote it said "I didn't like the ending." Funnily enough nor did I, but real life isn't always about happy endings, it is about happy moments before you eventually get to the end. I wanted to end this book when Danilo became mayor – that didn't happen. I wanted to end it with him being a lawyer – he isn't there yet although not that long to go, or when I became a Dominican citizen – that also hasn't happened yet due to Dominican bureaucracy. So there is no ending, just life goes on.

As I write this last chapter it is Sunday. Danilo has just finished his semester at university and the exam results are being published. He has a mental block when it comes to maths and for the last four years has struggled to pass the third maths exam to such an extent that he has put off attempting it for the last three years. But he has to pass to qualify, so this semester he bit the bullet. Unbelievably, and with a lot of help from me, we have just discovered he has passed.

Last week the fish man came to call. Fish man must be between seventy and eighty and once a week he goes on his clapped out motorbike to Puerto Plata to meet with the fishermen and fill up his cooler, which is precariously balanced on the back of the bike. It takes two hours to drive there so no idea how long it takes him. He has a hut in Los Pinos, on the road to Monción, and that is where we used to buy fish, but about four months ago he disappeared. No one knew where he was, just that his wife had left him, and I was told that Dominican men go off the rails when their wives leave. It was sad, as he had just started to call in here on his way back from Puerto Plata and we would always buy some fish from him.

Anyway, last week there was the sound of a motorbike at the gate, and someone shouted so I wandered outside, and there was fish man. He explained he had fallen off his bike and we had to look at the scars, and his wife left him and men cannot live alone so he had had to bring his ninety-year-old mother on the bike to his hut to look after him. He had spotted a massive six-pound snapper and knew it was our favourite so bought it for us. We took it and decided we would save it until Danilo passed maths, so today is the day, and eldest stepson Dany has arrived to help us eat it. On Sundays people always turn up, but we never know when or how many so we always cook a lot just in case.

I got up as usual around seven, and put the hot water on before wandering downstairs in my dressing gown and letting the dogs out. Put the coffee on, fed the cats and turned on the computer. I opened the windows and patio doors, so the outside comes inside. The sun was filtering through the mahogany wood at the back of the house and there was still a cool edge to the air. The flowers were glorious in the back garden, pink hibiscus, and vermillion red ginger plant, along with roses, purple vines and a whole range of different bougainvillea. The birds were up and about and the chickens and cockerels were making their way to the back of the house ready for Danilo to feed them. This time of the day was lovely and Danilo and Albert were still asleep so I could answer emails and check Facebook and forums.

Danilo got up and took the defrosted giant snapper and began to season it, while I started to do the washing in the twin tub washing machine. Washing was a pain as you have to fill with water, wash, drain, fill again, rinse, drain, spin and then go outside and hang everything on the barbed wire fence. Danilo then went to chop wood for the barbecue to cook the fish. The simple day-to-day tasks I loved, him doing some things and me doing others and in between I would work and write and he would study.

Life is full of choices. Some people, I assume, manage to drift through life without having to make major choices, but every day I come across people who have massive life-changing decisions to make. All of those ladies who decide to marry Dominican men even though it is often against the advice of their families and friends, but they have found someone who gives them the love they have always been seeking, even though they try and think the cultural and language barriers can be overcome. They can, but it is not always easy. Many did not agree with my decision to marry Danilo, but I would do it again in a heartbeat.

I remember talking to my grandmother when she was in her nineties and she told me that she was no longer living for herself, she only lived for the pleasure her grandchildren gave her. I have no children and no grandchildren, but the pleasure I have from watching others close to me grow and flourish is immeasurable. Watching Danilo, a man who had never been to school, who managed not only to pass his High School Leaving Certificate through home study, but also to get into university and do well, do very well, and who will soon qualify as a lawyer is amazing.

Watching Chivirico grow day by day and seeing how he brings joy to everyone he comes into contact with is something very special. And my step granddaughter, knowing what I could teach her in the future, and laughing at her as she chatters away is also lovely. And Albert, who knows if we can turn this damaged child around, but maybe, just maybe, he could be a baseball player and effectively a street kid who could have a future.

When I interviewed students who wanted to do an MBA, when I was a marketing lecturer in my former life, I would ask them what they wanted written on their gravestones. I know what I want. "She made a difference." Simple as that. When you have no children, no way of leaving your genes behind when you go, you need to be here for a reason, to know your life has meaning and some different measure of immortality. Not purely to exist. I need to know I am here for a reason; I need to know that my life has meaning, that I can pass on something, anything, to other people and help them to make more of their lives. This is the perfect place to do that.

Do I regret my choice to come to the Dominican Republic? No, never. Do I regret staying and marrying Danilo? No, never. I miss my mother and my sister, although I speak to Mum on Skype every day, and I have no idea if I will ever see them again as, until I have citizenship (I am still waiting after two years for my Interpol report) I cannot leave. And even then I will have to find the fare and a visa for Danilo as I am not going without him.

I love the simplicity of the life we have in Wasp House, love cooking and making things from scratch and watching the trees in the garden grow – we may even have our first avocados on our very own tree this year. Seeing pizza or bread dough rise, almost oozing out of the bowl. Watching baby chickens with their mum as I throw them bread and mum breaks it up for them to eat. Watching big, fat green lizards catch flies and mosquitos and watching the dogs jump excitedly along the track when we take them for a walk. Walking to the *colmado*, saying hello to people along the way and calling in at Angela's on the way back for a coffee and a natter. She always gives me something to bring home, an avocado or two, or yuca or a bunch of bananas – as she says, "God gives to those who give to others." Chatting to friends online and the pleasure of receiving an email from a stranger saying they loved the book and were kind enough to take the time to write. Every few months going to Santo Domingo or Sosúa and leaving the house I leave so rarely, and eating in a restaurant, or shopping in a proper supermarket. All of these things I love, which most people would take for granted.

Is it hard living here? Yes, it is sometimes, as you have read. Losing valued and much loved pets for no good reason.

Being without water sometimes, being without money many times. We have no loans, no credit cards, no lines of credit. When the money is there it is there, but when it goes there is nothing. In the case of emergency my mother, sister or Shirley or other friends step in. And my family and friends have been my lifeline on more than one occasion for which I will be eternally grateful.

People talk about their holidays and going out. Danilo and I have not been out to dance, to a restaurant, or on holiday together for years. We went to Barahona in 2014 and to Ro's birthday party in Sosúa two years ago. So much for 'date nights' but it doesn't really matter. We are still amazingly happy.

Do I regret Danilo running for mayor? I regret the lost money of course, but I cannot regret letting him follow his dream and the dreams of many more. Most people here only have their dreams, they are what keeps them going. Do I regret the choice to move to Wasp House? No never. It isn't easy all the time, but most of the people are the salt of the earth and every minute of every day I appreciate the view, living in the countryside, and always feeling safe.

And when I look at what is happening around the world I am so grateful and so glad I am here. A different kind of stress, far less pressure, living with the simple things in life. Yes, there is corruption, although I am not sure if there's more than other places, maybe just more obvious. Yes, there is poverty and much more than many other countries, but when I eventually take the oath to be a Dominican citizen, which will happen one day soon I hope, I will be proud that this country and these people have taken me in as one of their own.

Life in the Dominican Republic gives you so much more than life in first world countries, and teaches you what is really important, but it also takes much more from you with the corruption, lack of affordable and knowledgeable health care, lack of care for animals, lack of veterinary support and lack of certain foods – especially living in the countryside. You have to decide what is important for you.

When I made the decision to leave England in 2001 I didn't know what I was looking for, but knew I would know when I found it. And I have been lucky enough to find it. I wish for you all, my friends, family, DR Sisterhood clients, readers of my books, the luck to find what you really want, the courage to keep looking for it until you find it, and the strength to overcome the obstacles along the way.

"Therefore be at peace with God, whatever you conceive him to be, and whatever your labours and aspirations, in the noisy confusion of life, keep peace with your soul."
Desiderata, Max Ehrmann, 1927

THE PLAYERS

FAMILY

Lindsay de Feliz
Danilo Feliz Torres – *her husband*
Dany Alberto Feliz Martinez – *Danilo's son living in Esperanza*
José Alberto Feliz Martinez – *Danilo's son living in Esperanza*
Ana – *his wife*
Adibel – *their daughter, Lindsay's step-granddaughter*
Christian Alberto Feliz Alvarez – *Danilo's son living in Spain*
Antonio – *Danilo's half brother*
Albert – *Antonio's son*
Shirley Firth – *Lindsay's mother*
Elisabeth and Gary Eastburn – *Lindsay's sister and her husband*

FOSTER CHILDREN

Eury – *a.k.a Chivirico*
Albert

DOMINICANS IN THE *CAMPO* IN CACIQU

Angela, *la bruja*, her husband, Leopoldo, and their son Christian
Miguel and his wife Barbara
Sukin and Leida
Feluche, his son Berto, daughter Margarita and her husband
Moreno and their two daughters

DWENDIES

Saya
Hector

EXPAT FRIENDS IN THE DOMINICAN REPUBLIC

Grace and Nany
Shirley
Rosanne
Jonathan

THE DOGS

Fred – *daughter of Can Can, Pitbull/ mongrel cross* (*deceased*)
Tyson – *Great Dane* (*deceased*)
Sophie – *daughter of Tyson and Fred* (*deceased*)
Silly Boy – *English Mastiff* (*deceased*)
Meg – *Rottweiler, Chow Chow cross*
Belinda – *Great Dane* (*deceased*)
Lobo – *Siberian Husky*
Panda and Pandora, Sweepy and Grita Mucho – *puppies of Meg and Lobo* (*deceased*)
Rin Tin Tin – *son of granddaughter of Meg and Lobo and a Belgian Shepherd* (*deceased*)
Canguru – *daughter of Lobo and Grita Mucho*

LIST OF PHOTOGRAPHS

DEDICATION

Danilo and Chivirico

CHAPTER 1

The pink house

CHAPTER 2

Chivirico at the bank

CHAPTER 3

The front of wasp house

CHAPTER 4

Traditional outdoor cooking stove (*fogon*)

CHAPTER 5

Car stuck on the hill in Barahona – photograph © Tracy Perez

CHAPTER 6

Chivirico and Monster the cockerel

CHAPTER 7

Tarantula in the shower

CHAPTER 8

Belinda the Great Dane

CHAPTER 9

Albert and Chivirico

CHAPTER 10

Danilo mixing concrete

All photographs © Lindsay de Feliz unless otherwise stated.

AUTHOR BIOGRAPHY

LINDSAY DE FELIZ WAS BORN, RAISED and educated in the UK, gaining a degree in French and German at Wolverhampton University, and an MBA at Bradford University. Following a successful career in marketing she decided to leave it all behind and follow her dreams.

Arriving in the Dominican Republic as a scuba diving instructor, for a six-month contract, she ended up staying and married a Dominican, becoming a stepmother to three young boys. She was then shot in her own home during a burglary and, following a long fight against corruption along with her husband, left the life of an expat in a tourist resort to live, first, in a Dominican town and then in the mountains.

Lindsay published the highly successful memoir, *What About Your Saucepans?* in 2013 – about the first ten years of her life in the Dominican Republic – and now lives high up in the Dominican mountains, on a small farm, with her husband Danilo, three dogs, two cats, one permanent and one temporary foster child and too many chickens to count. She works as a writer, translator and marketing consultant.

Lindsay writes a blog about the Dominican Republic and daily life at: www.yoursaucepans.blogspot.com

Twitter: @lindsaydefeliz

Email: yoursaucepans@hotmail.com

Facebook: What about your saucepans? and DRsisterhood

PASSAGE OF THE STORK

DELIVERING THE SOUL

One woman's journey
to self-realization
and acceptance

MADELEINE LENAGH

Also Published by summertimepublishing

CHRISTOPHER O'SHAUGHNESSY

Available from expatbookshop.com

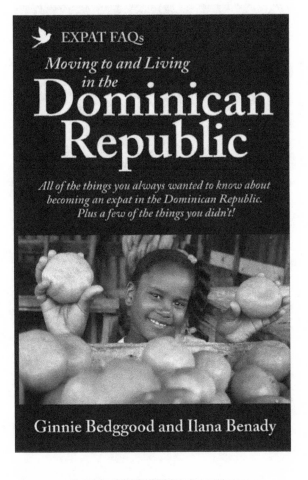

EXPAT FAQs

Moving to and Living in the

Dominican Republic

*All of the things you always wanted to know about
becoming an expat in the Dominican Republic.
Plus a few of the things you didn't!*

Ginnie Bedggood and Ilana Benady

THE EMOTIONALLY RESILIENT EXPAT

Engage, Adapt and Thrive Across Cultures

"Groundbreaking..."
Ruth E. Van Reken
Author of *Third Culture Kids*

LINDA A. JANSSEN

CPSIA information can be obtained
at www.ICGtesting.com
Printed in the USA
LVHW042233120120
643229LV00003B/570/P

9 780995 502741